HOW TO DRAW BATMAN, SUPERMAN,

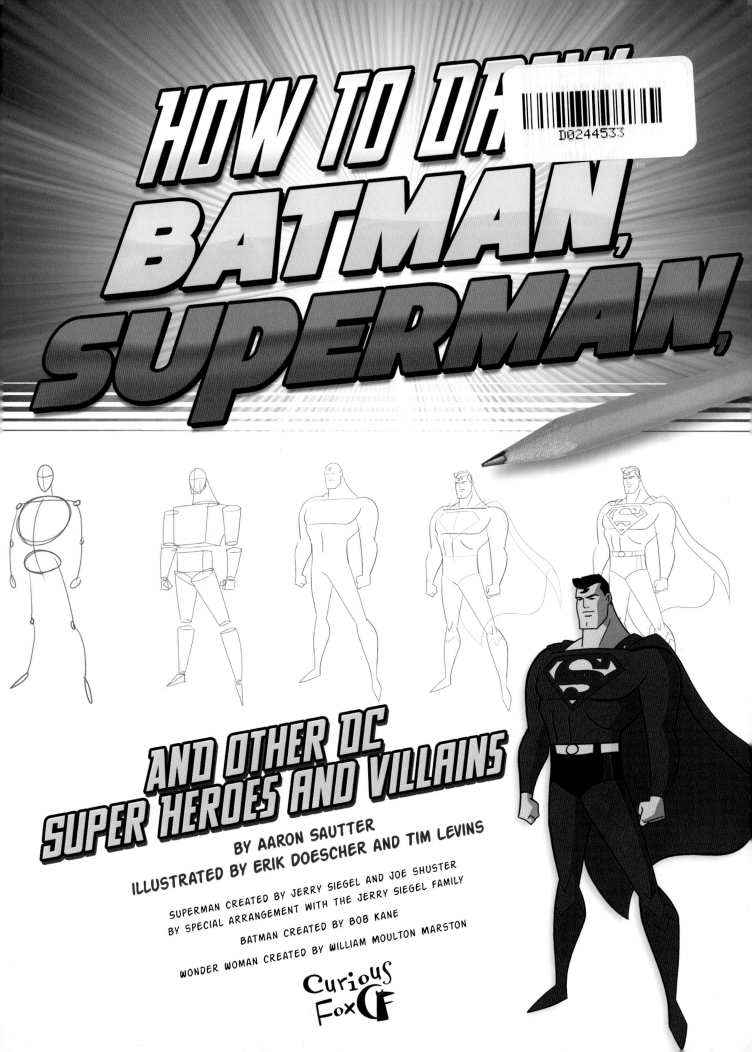

AND OTHER DC SUPER HEROES AND VILLAINS

BY AARON SAUTTER

ILLUSTRATED BY ERIK DOESCHER AND TIM LEVINS

SUPERMAN CREATED BY JERRY SIEGEL AND JOE SHUSTER
BY SPECIAL ARRANGEMENT WITH THE JERRY SIEGEL FAMILY

BATMAN CREATED BY BOB KANE

WONDER WOMAN CREATED BY WILLIAM MOULTON MARSTON

Curious Fox

TABLE OF CONTENTS

Let's Draw Incredible DC Super Heroes and Villains!

The forces of evil are on the move and villains are plotting to take over the world. Who can people turn to in this dark hour? Super heroes!

Do you enjoy seeing Batman outwit the Joker? Do you like watching Superman defeat Lex Luthor's evil plans? Maybe you enjoy stories about Wonder Woman, Green Lantern, and The Flash as they defend the Earth. Or maybe you just enjoy rooting against bad guys like Sinestro, Cheetah, Black Manta, or Captain Cold.

The DC Universe is filled with hundreds of colourful heroes and villains - and now you can draw your favourites! This book is packed with fun drawing projects to get you started. Want to draw Superman and his Fortress of Solitude? Want to draw Batman and his Batmobile? Those are here, along with dozens of other super heroes and their foes!

What are you waiting for? Gather your supplies and sharpen your pencils. Then turn the page and start sketching your favorite DC Super Heroes and Super-Villains!

WHAT YOU'LL NEED

You don't need superpowers to draw mighty heroes. But you'll need some basic tools. Gather the following stationery before starting your amazing art.

PAPER: You can get special drawing paper from art and craft shops. But any type of blank, unlined paper will be fine.

PENCILS: Drawings should be done in pencil first. Even professionals use them. If you make a mistake, it'll be easy to rub out and redraw. Keep plenty of these essential drawing tools on hand.

PENCIL SHARPENER: To make clean lines, you need to keep your pencils sharp. Get a good pencil sharpener. You'll use it a lot.

ERASERS: As you draw, you're bound to make mistakes. Erasers give artists the power to turn back time and rub out those mistakes. Get some high quality rubber or kneaded erasers. They'll last a lot longer than pencil erasers.

BLACK FELT-TIP PENS: When your drawing is ready, trace over the final lines with black felt-tip pen. The dark lines will help to make your characters stand out on the page.

COLOURED PENCILS AND PENS: Ready to finish your masterpiece? Bring your characters to life and give them some colour with coloured pencils or pens.

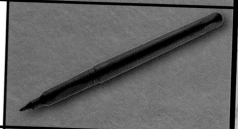

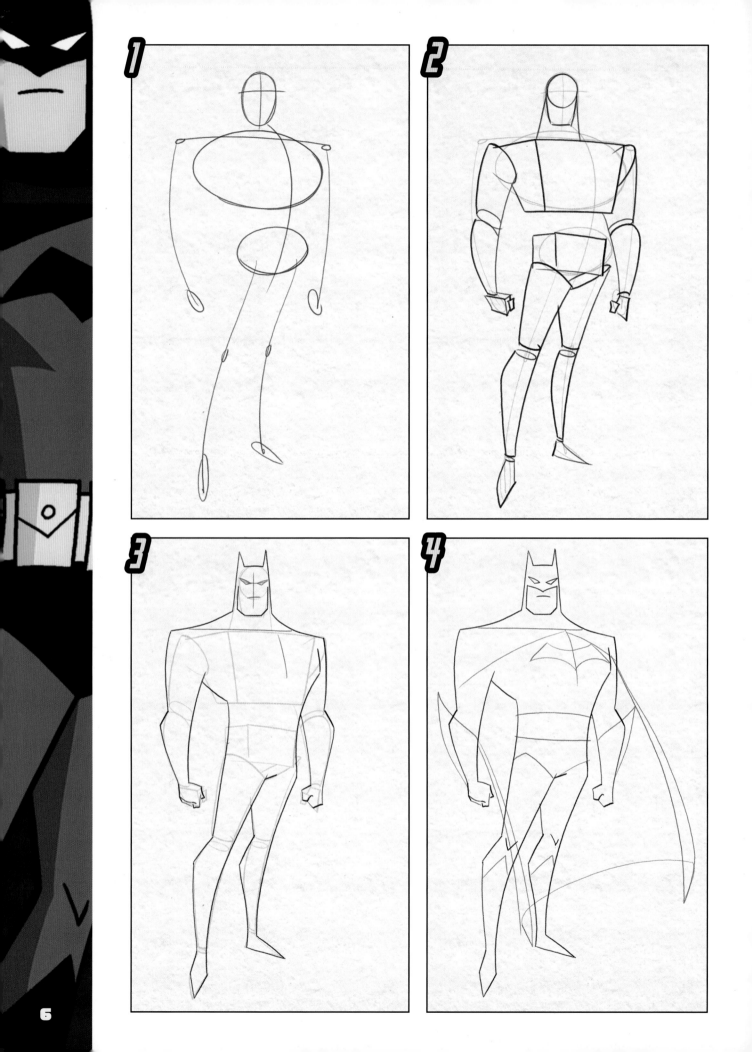

1

2

3

4

BATSUIT

Batman wouldn't be Batman without his Batsuit. The suit's main purpose is to hide Bruce Wayne's identity, while striking terror into the hearts of criminals. The suit also helps Batman to hide in the shadows as he prowls through the night. Batman's Utility Belt holds his many crime-fighting tools, including Batarangs, a grapnel, binoculars and remote controls for his vehicles.

BATCAVE

Sometimes the World's Greatest Detective needs a quiet place to think. When Batman needs answers, he goes to his secret Batcave. There, he uses the powerful Batcomputer to study clues and find the information he needs. The Batcave is also home to Batman's amazing vehicles and the workshop where he creates his incredible crime-fighting gadgets.

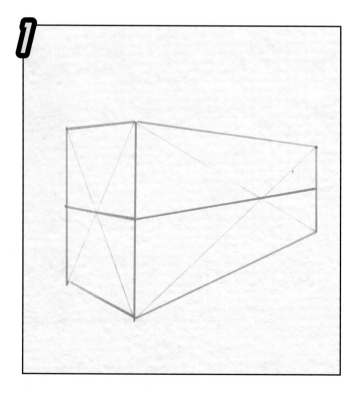

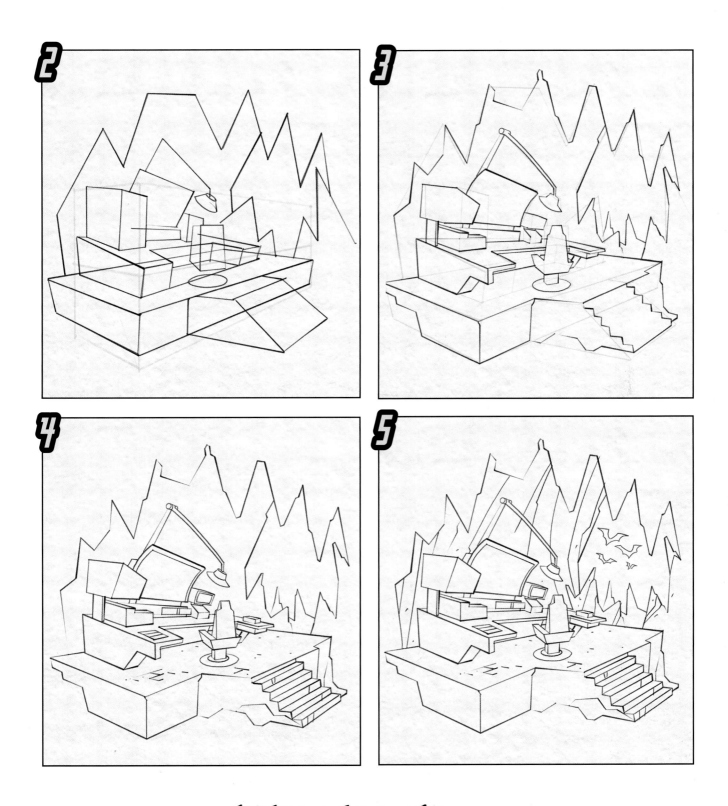

DRAWING IDEA
Next try drawing the Batmobile blasting out of the Batcave's secret entrance!

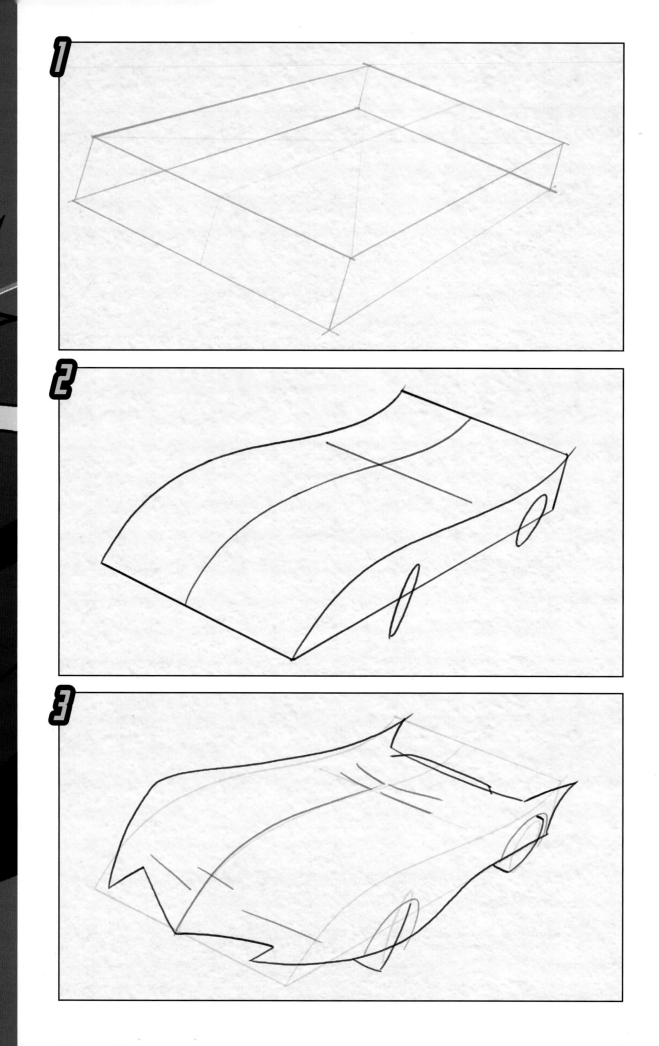

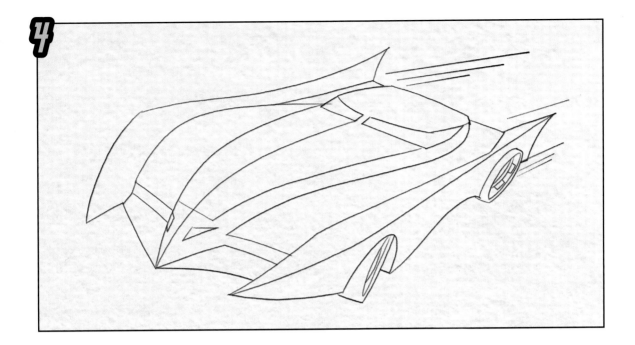

BATMOBILE

When Batman needs to be somewhere fast, he relies on the Batmobile to get him there. With its jet-powered engine, this speedy car helps Batman to get across Gotham City in a flash. Batman also uses the Batmobile to chase down villains in their getaway cars. This armoured car is equipped with grappling hooks and road spikes. It can also create slippery oil slicks to stop criminals from escaping.

DRAWING IDEA
Try drawing the Batmobile chasing Two-Face's getaway car after a bank robbery!

FIGHTING CRIME

Criminals in Gotham City don't stand a chance with Batman around. He's always on the lookout for thugs trying to break the law. When a super-villain like Bane tries to rob a bank, the Dark Knight is on the case. Bane is very intelligent and has superhuman strength. But Batman's fighting skills and experience can stop the master criminal in his tracks!

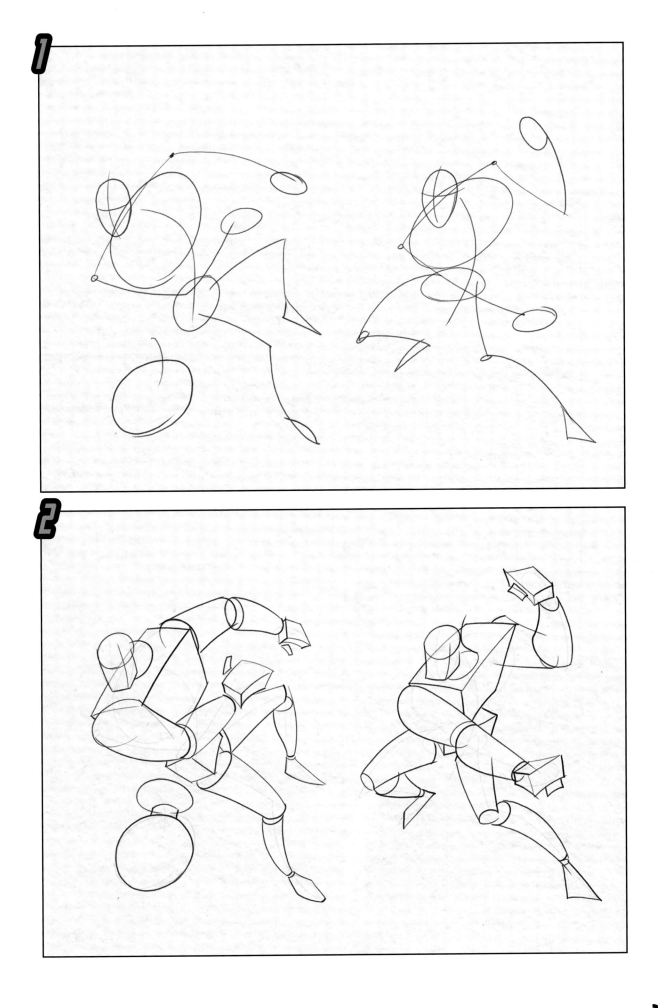

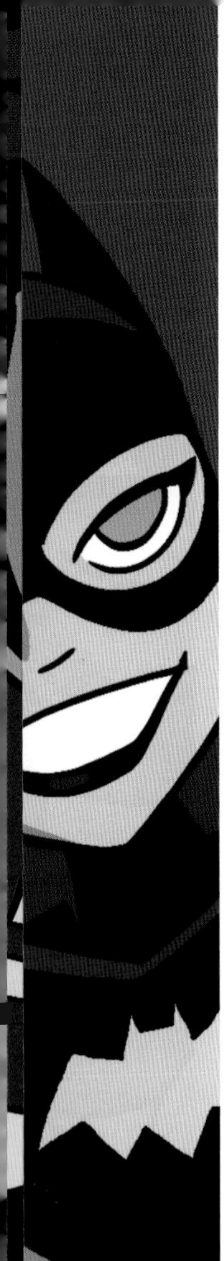

1

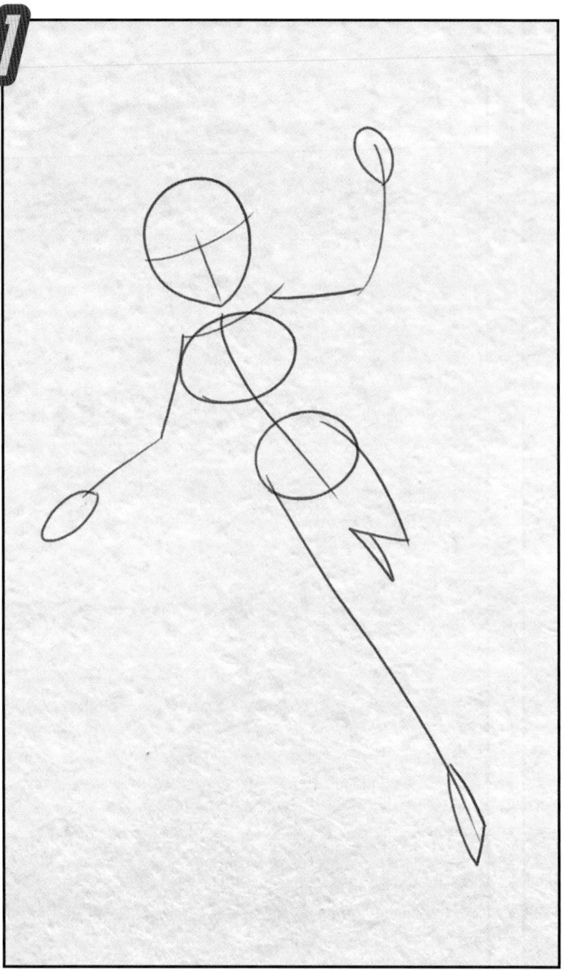

2

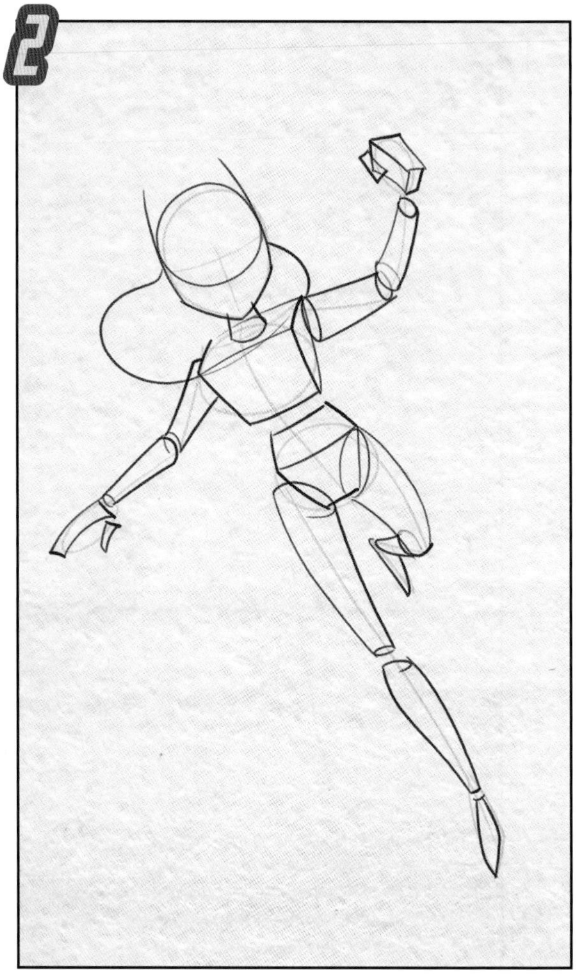

3

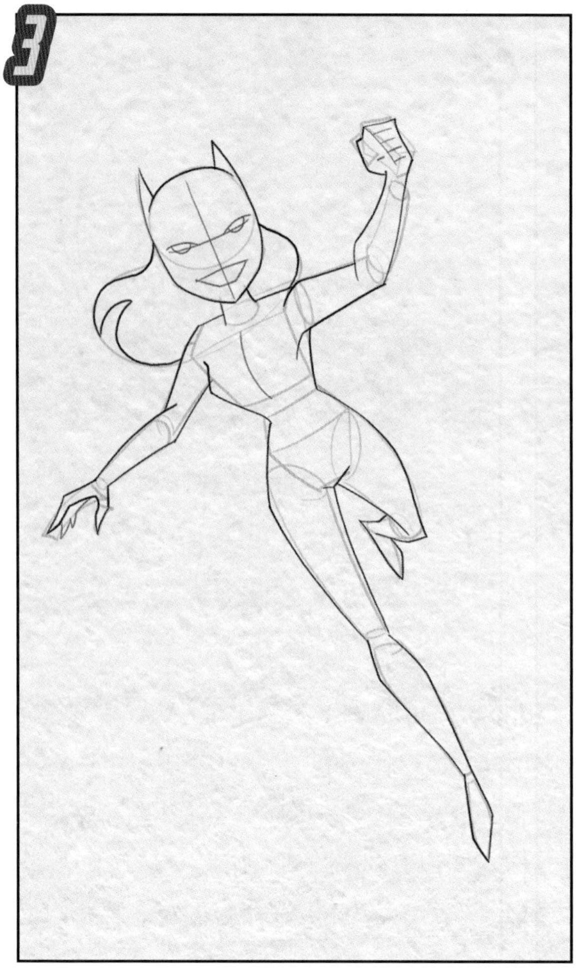

4

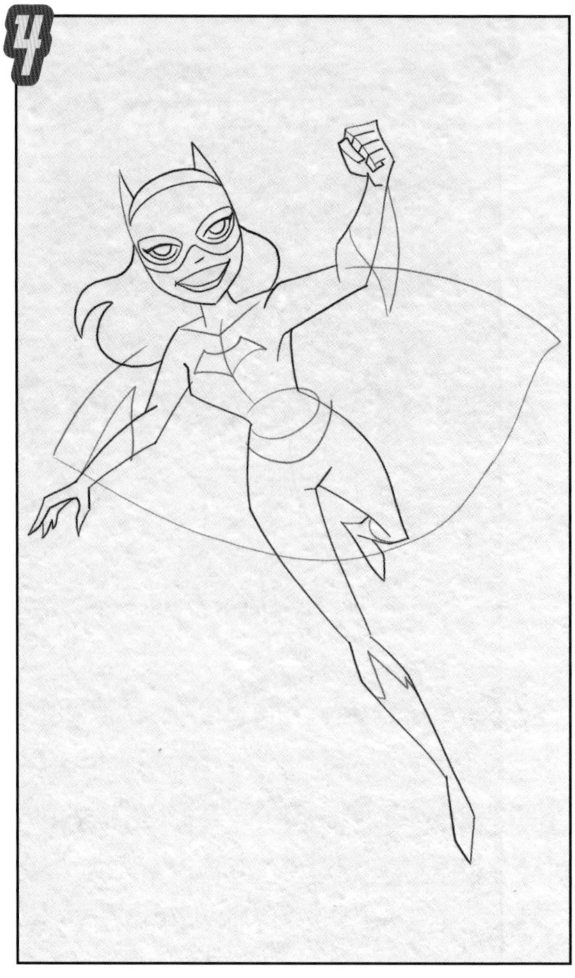

5

DRAWING IDEA
Try drawing Batgirl working with Robin to track down the Penguin and his thugs!

BATGIRL

Real Name: Barbara Gordon

Home Base: Gotham City

Occupation: college student, crime fighter

Abilities: gymnastics, martial arts skills

Background: Barbara Gordon takes after her father, Police Commissioner James Gordon. She is strong-willed and dedicated to wiping out crime from Gotham City. When Barbara's father was framed for a crime he didn't commit, she made her own bat-themed suit and attempted to break him out of jail. Since then Batgirl has become part of Batman's team, helping him to defend Gotham City from crime.

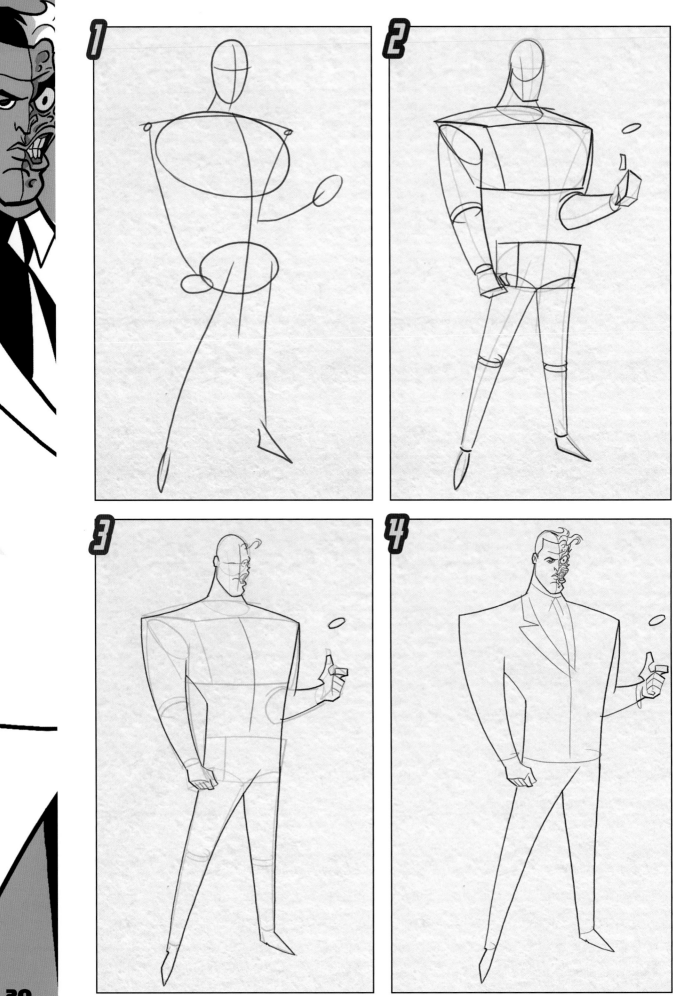

TWO-FACE

Real Name: Harvey Dent
Home Base: Gotham City
Occupation: professional criminal
Enemy of: Batman
Abilities: above-average strength and fighting skills, expert marksmanship
Equipment: special two-headed coin to make most decisions

Background: Harvey Dent was once the best lawyer in Gotham City. He worked tirelessly to send the city's most dangerous criminals to jail. But when an explosion scarred half of his face and body, Harvey's darker side took control. He became the criminal Two-Face. Now he tries to run the same criminal world he once fought so hard to bring to justice.

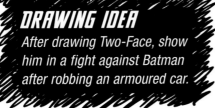

DRAWING IDEA
After drawing Two-Face, show him in a fight against Batman after robbing an armoured car.

1

THE RIDDLER

Real Name: Edward Nygma

Home Base: Gotham City

Occupation: professional criminal

Enemy of: Batman

Abilities: genius intellect

Equipment: question-mark cane containing hidden weapons and gadgets

Background: Edward Nygma loved riddles and puzzles as a boy. When he grew up he invented a popular video game called *Riddle of the Minotaur.* The game sold millions of copies, but Nygma never received a penny for his work. To get his revenge, he became the genius criminal the Riddler. He enjoys leaving cryptic clues to his crimes. Only Batman can solve the Riddler's puzzling crimes and put a stop to his wicked plans.

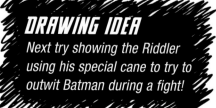

DRAWING IDEA
Next try showing the Riddler using his special cane to try to outwit Batman during a fight!

26

STOPPING THE JOKER

The Joker loves being Batman's arch-enemy. He's always hoping to get the better of the Dark Knight. The Joker enjoys designing weapons with a comical look to hide their true danger. For example, a huge bomb filled with deadly Joker Venom might look like a big party toy. But Batman is very familiar with how the Clown Prince of Crime thinks. He's always ready to swoop into action and put a stop to the Joker's plans before innocent people get hurt.

SUPERMAN'S SUIT

When Clark arrived on Earth from Krypton, he was wrapped in blue and red blankets. Martha Kent used the blankets to create Superman's suit and cape. The Man of Steel doesn't wear a mask with his outfit. He wants to earn people's trust and show that he has nothing to hide.

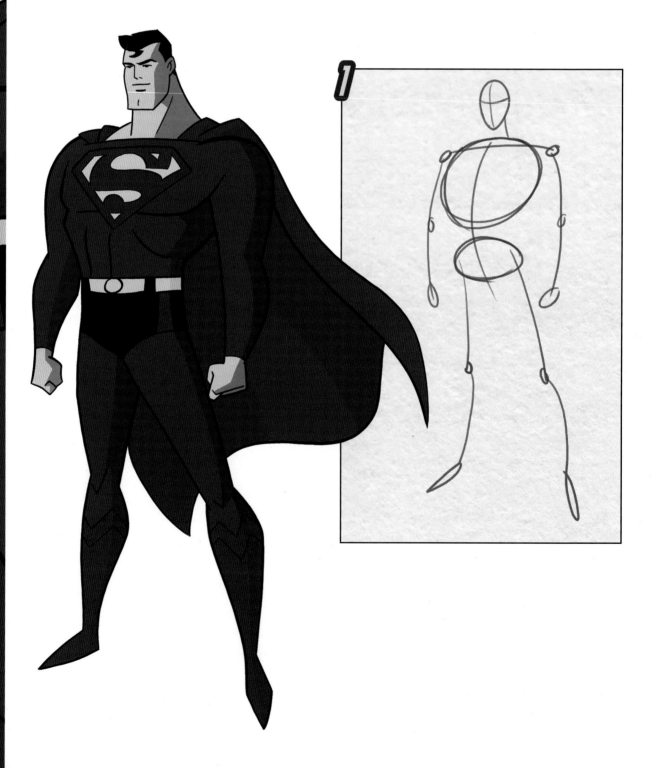

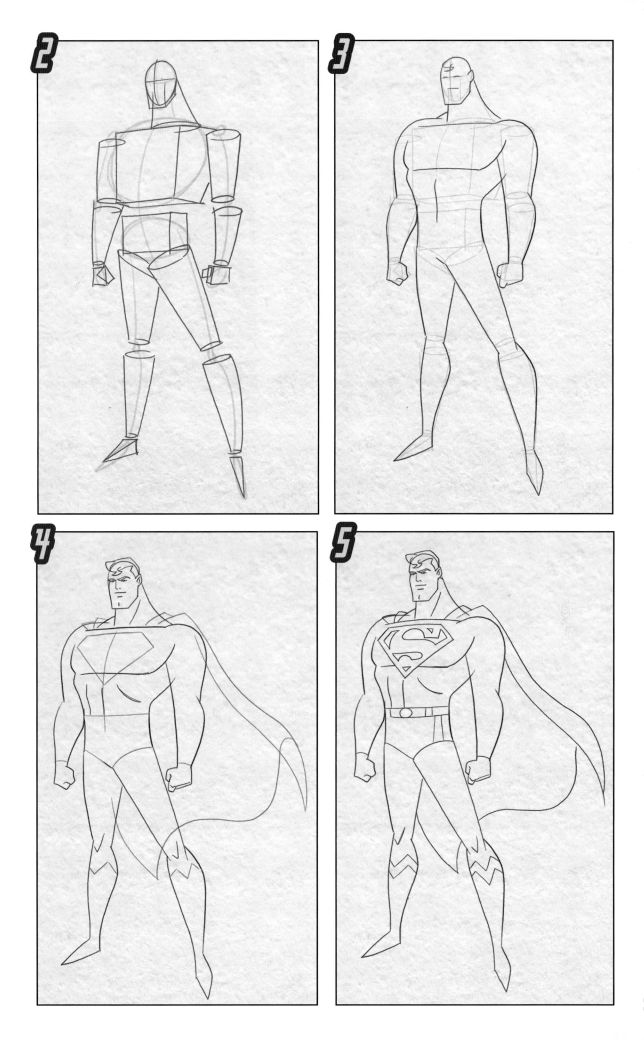

FORTRESS OF SOLITUDE

Superman normally calls Metropolis home. But when he needs time to himself, he goes to his secret Fortress of Solitude in the Arctic. There is only one door into the fortress, which is always locked. Only Superman has the strength needed to lift the giant metal key that unlocks the fortress door.

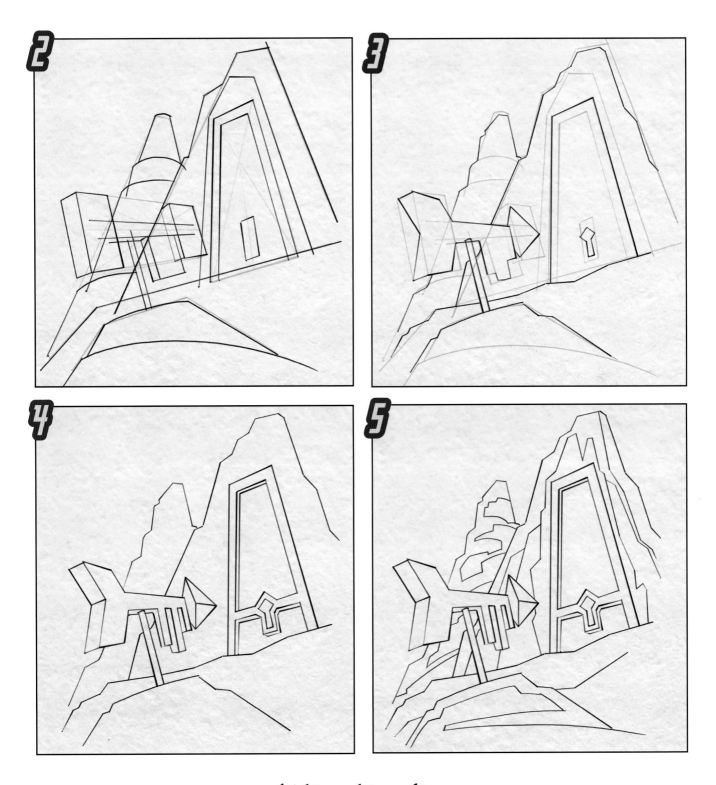

DRAWING IDEA
Next try to draw Superman
lifting the key to open the
Fortress door!

HEAT VISION

1

Heat vision is one of Superman's most powerful and useful abilities. He can use it to smash rocks or blast through concrete walls. Superman can also focus this power and use it like a laser beam. He often uses this ability to cut through steel plates or weld objects together to save people in danger.

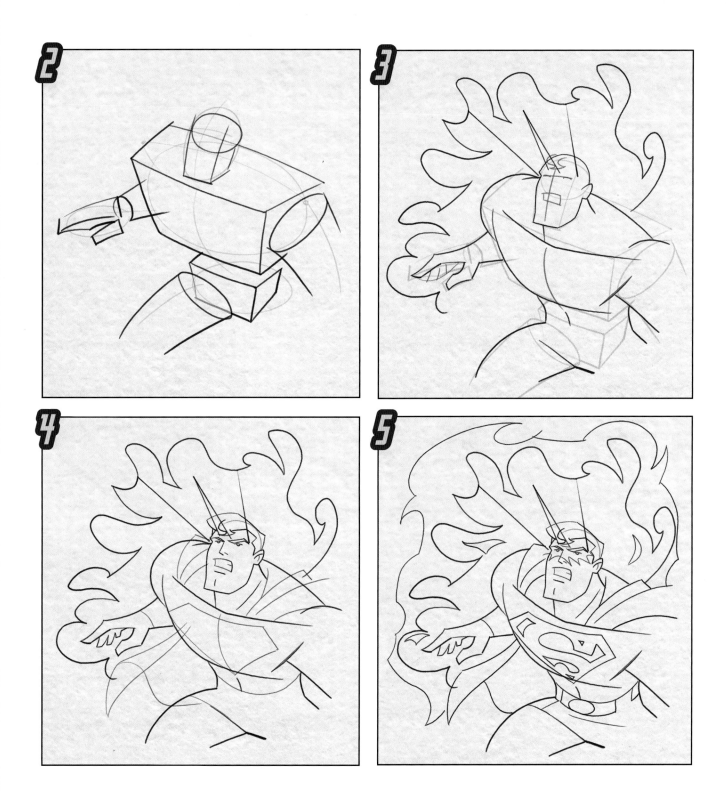

DRAWING IDEA

Try drawing Superman blasting through a rock wall with his heat vision!

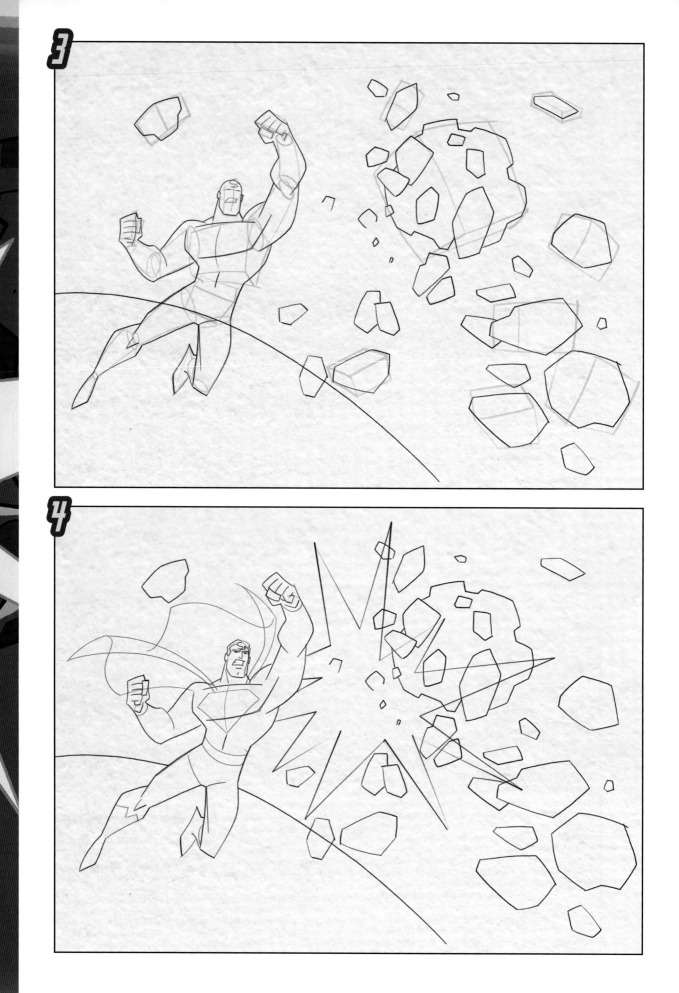

DAILY PLANET FRIENDS

Names: Lois Lane and Jimmy Olsen

Home Base: Daily Planet Building, Metropolis

Occupation: reporter; photographer

Abilities: strong investigation skills

Background: Everybody needs a few good friends, including the Man of Steel. Clark's closest friends work with him at the *Daily Planet.* Jimmy is a photographer and often gets the best photos of Superman. Lois works closely with Clark to cover the biggest news stories in Metropolis.

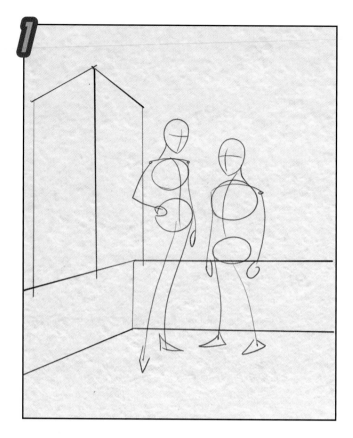

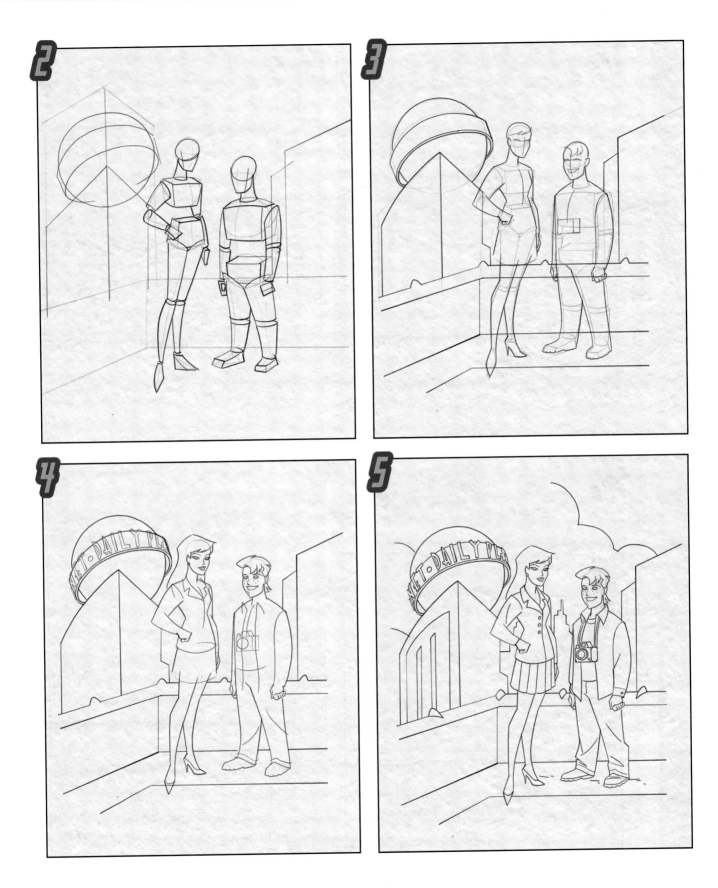

DRAWING IDEA
Now try drawing Clark, Lois and Jimmy covering a major story in downtown Metropolis.

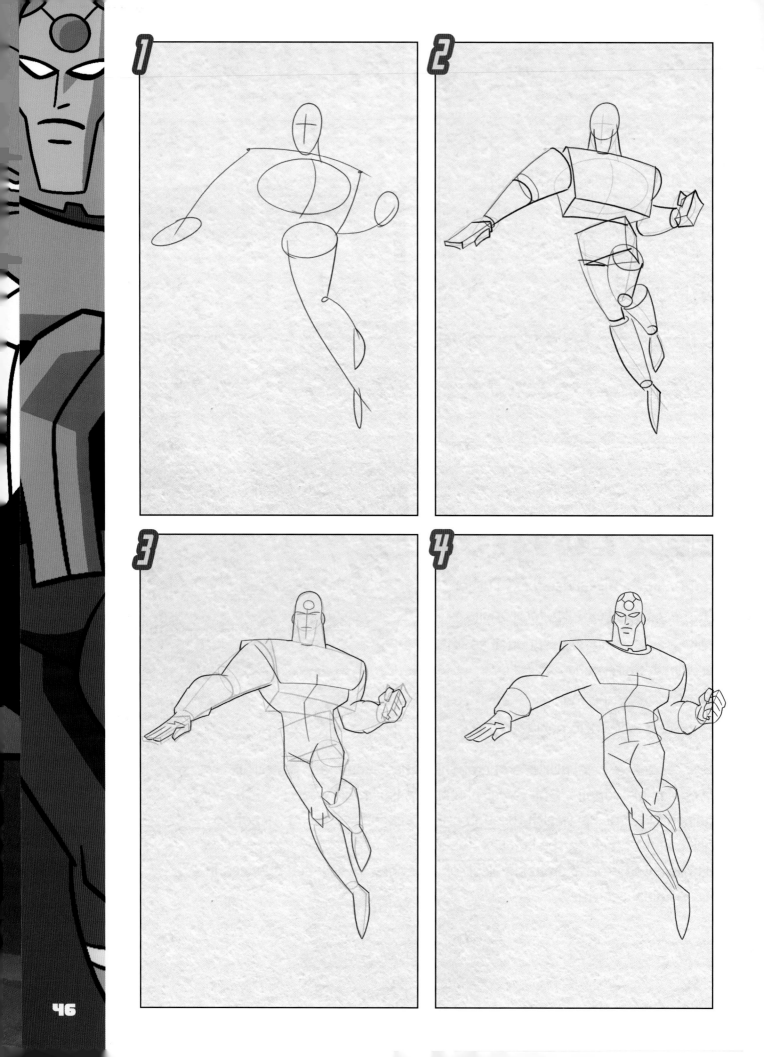

BRAINIAC

Real Name: unknown

Home Base: Skull Ship

Occupation: super-villain

Enemy of: Superman

Abilities: genius intellect, enhanced strength, flight, master of technology

Background: Brainiac was once a powerful computer on Krypton. It became so intelligent that it became self-aware and left the planet before it was destroyed. Now Brainiac travels the universe, destroying countless planets to harvest their technologies. Brainiac can take control of most forms of technology and uses its vast knowledge to outsmart anyone who stands in its way. Only Superman can match the wits and strength of this walking, talking computer.

DRAWING IDEA
Next try drawing Brainiac's powerful skull-shaped spaceship!

BIZARRO

Real Name: unknown

Home Base: Bizarro World

Occupation: super-villain

Enemy of: Superman

Abilities: super-strength, flight, freeze vision, fire breath

Background: Bizarro is a twisted clone of Superman created by Lex Luthor. Bizarro's powers are equal but opposite to Superman's. For example, instead of fiery heat vision, Bizarro blasts beams of ice from his eyes. He is also unpredictable and doesn't know his own strength — making him a dangerous threat to Metropolis.

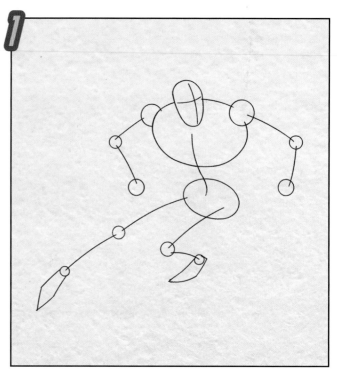

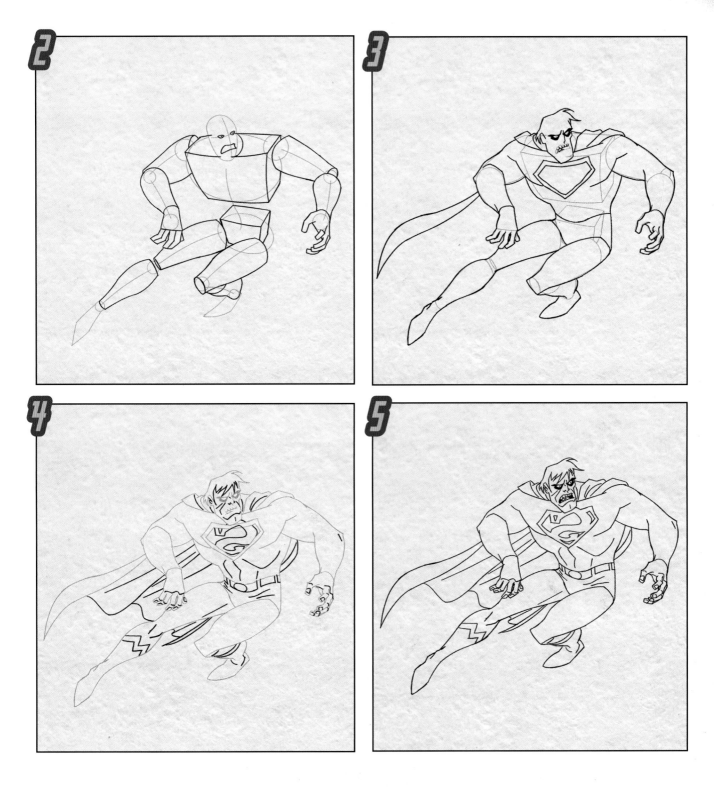

DRAWING IDEA

Try drawing Bizarro saving a cat stuck in a tree — by pulling the tree out of the ground!

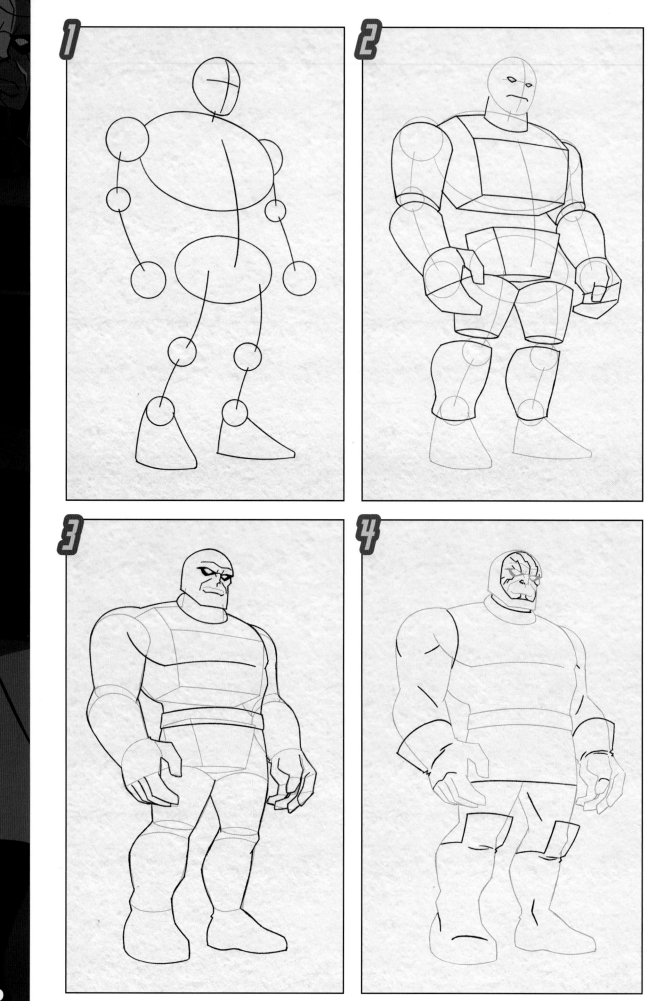

DARKSEID

Real Name: Uxas

Home Base: Apokolips

Occupation: dictator and tyrant, New God

Enemy of: Superman

Abilities: superhuman strength, speed and stamina; invulnerability; immortality; genius intellect; telepathy; mind control; Omega Beams

Background: Darkseid rules over the planet Apokolips with an iron fist. But he also plans to rule the entire universe! Darkseid has limitless strength and can blast his enemies with deadly Omega Beams from his eyes. Only Superman has the strength to truly weaken or injure him. With his unmatched power, Darkseid is nothing less than the most dangerous enemy in the known universe.

DRAWING IDEA
Next draw Darkseid as he tries to defeat the Man of Steel with his deadly Omega Beams!

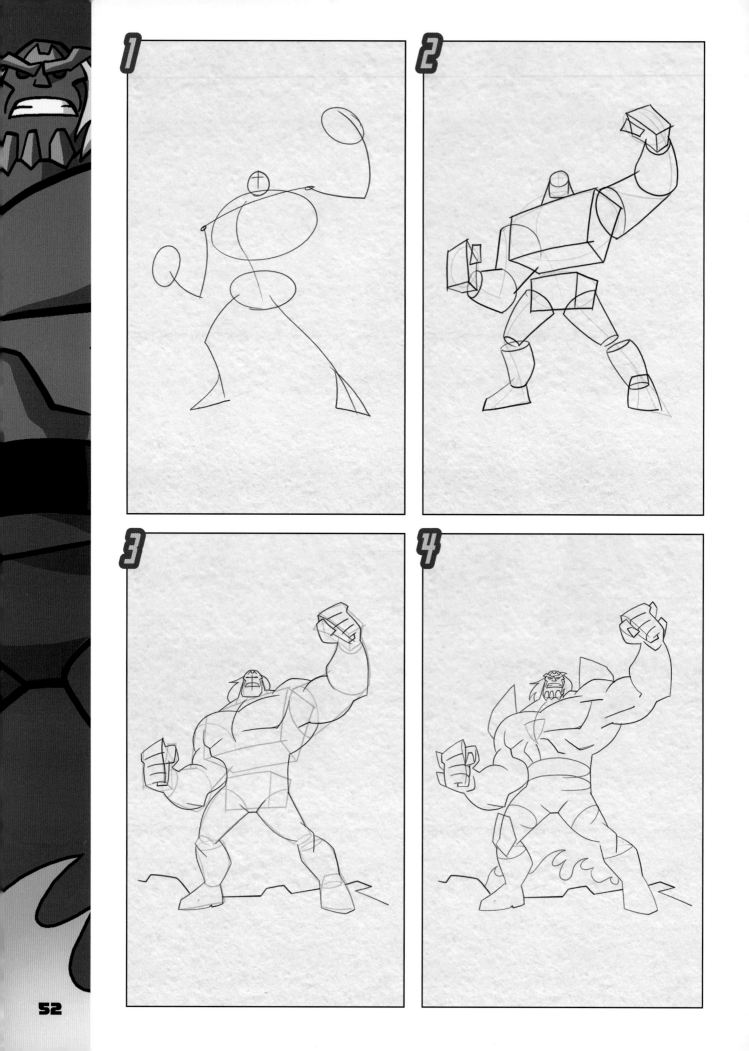

DOOMSDAY

Real Name: Doomsday

Home Base: Krypton

Occupation: destroyer

Enemy of: Superman

Abilities: super-strength and speed; regeneration; invincibility

Background: Doomsday is an indestructible force of rage. He desires only to destroy everything in his path. This creature is almost impossible to stop. If he dies, he just comes back to life stronger than before — and immune to whatever killed him! Doomsday's body is covered with sharp, jagged bones that he uses as both armour and dangerous weapons. His superpowers and violent nature make Doomsday one of the Man of Steel's deadliest foes.

DRAWING IDEA
After drawing Doomsday, try drawing him in a major battle with the Man of Steel!

GENERAL ZOD

Real Name: Dru-Zod

Home Base: Krypton

Occupation: criminal warlord

Enemy of: Superman

Abilities: super-strength, speed and breath; heat vision; flight; invincibility

Background: General Zod was a military leader who tried to take over Krypton, but failed. As punishment, Zod and his followers were banished to the mysterious Phantom Zone. When they escaped, Zod decided that he would rule over Earth instead of Krypton. Luckily, Superman is there to stop Zod and his evil plans. However, Zod's powers match those of Superman. Defeating this warrior from Krypton will be the Man of Steel's greatest challenge.

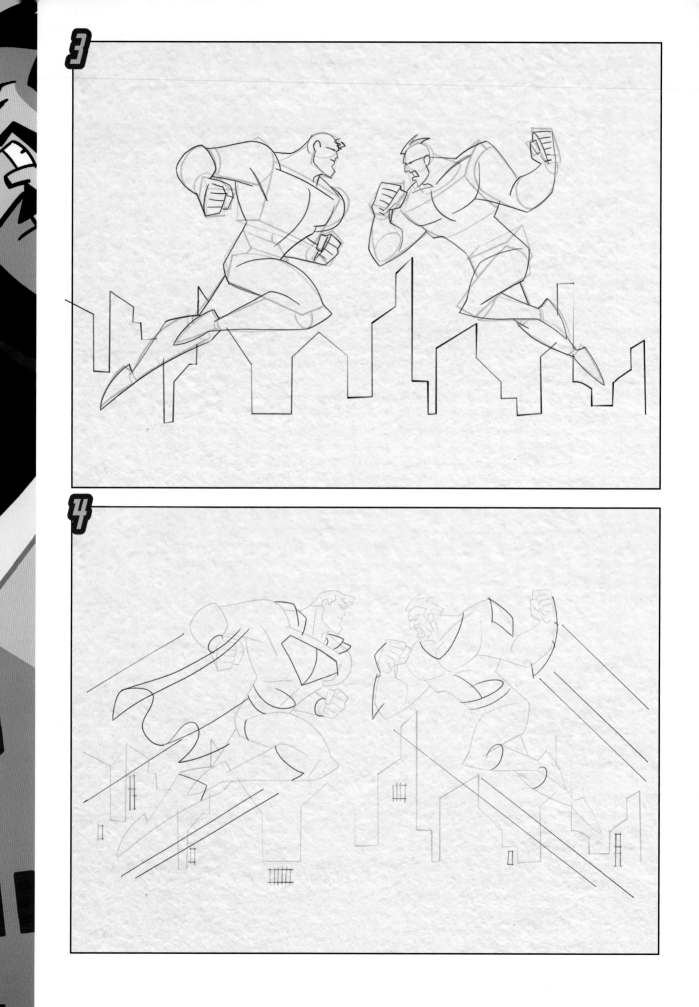

THE JOKER

Real Name: unknown

Home Base: Gotham City

Occupation: professional criminal

Enemy of: Batman

Abilities: above-average strength, genius-level intellect, skills in chemistry and engineering

Background: Also known as the Clown Prince of Crime, the Joker is Batman's most dangerous enemy. When he fell into a vat of toxic waste, he was transformed into an evil madman. The chemicals bleached his skin white, dyed his hair green and peeled his lips back into a permanent, hideous grin. The Joker delights in tormenting Batman and the innocent people of Gotham City.

DRAWING IDEA
Try drawing the Joker with a deadly hand buzzer or other practical joke device.

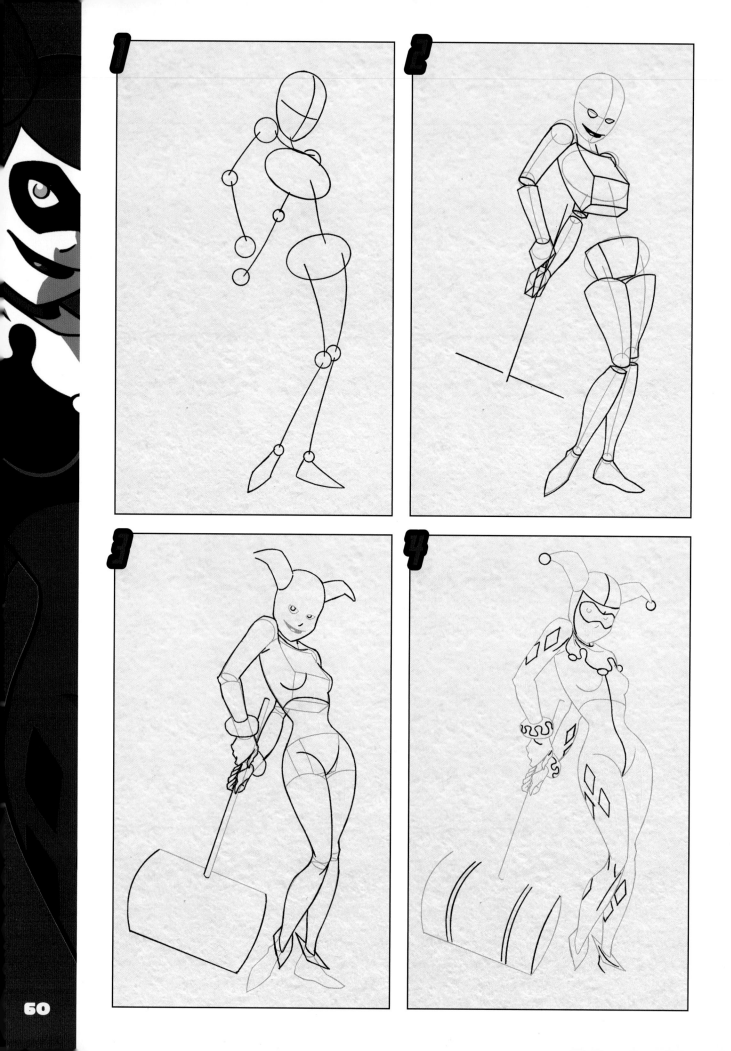

HARLEY QUINN

Real Name: Dr. Harleen Quinzel

Home Base: Gotham City

Occupation: psychiatrist, professional criminal

Enemy of: Batman

Abilities: Olympic-level gymnast and acrobat

Equipment: giant mallet

Background: Dr. Harleen Quinzel was once a successful psychiatrist at Gotham City's Arkham Asylum. But when she met the Joker everything changed. When the Joker told Harley the heartbreaking, but false, story of his troubled childhood, her heart was won over. Harley fell in love with the Joker and soon helped him to escape. She now clowns around Gotham City as Harley Quinn, the Joker's girlfriend and partner in crime.

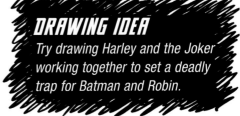

DRAWING IDEA
Try drawing Harley and the Joker working together to set a deadly trap for Batman and Robin.

BANE

Real Name: unknown

Home Base: Gotham City

Occupation: assassin and professional criminal

Enemy of: Batman

Abilities: superhuman strength, genius-level intellect

Equipment: Venom drug

Background: Bane's background is a mystery, even to Batman. The only thing known for sure is that Bane was once a prisoner. He was chosen as a test subject for a new drug called Venom. The drug gave Bane superhuman strength. He now uses it to stay strong and works as one of Gotham City's criminal masterminds. Bane's greatest desire is to be the one person who can defeat the Dark Knight — permanently.

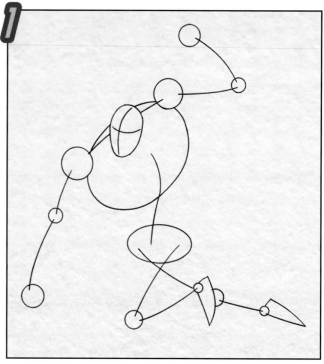

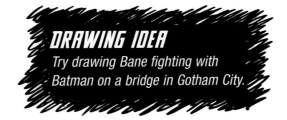

DRAWING IDEA

*Try drawing Bane fighting with
Batman on a bridge in Gotham City.*

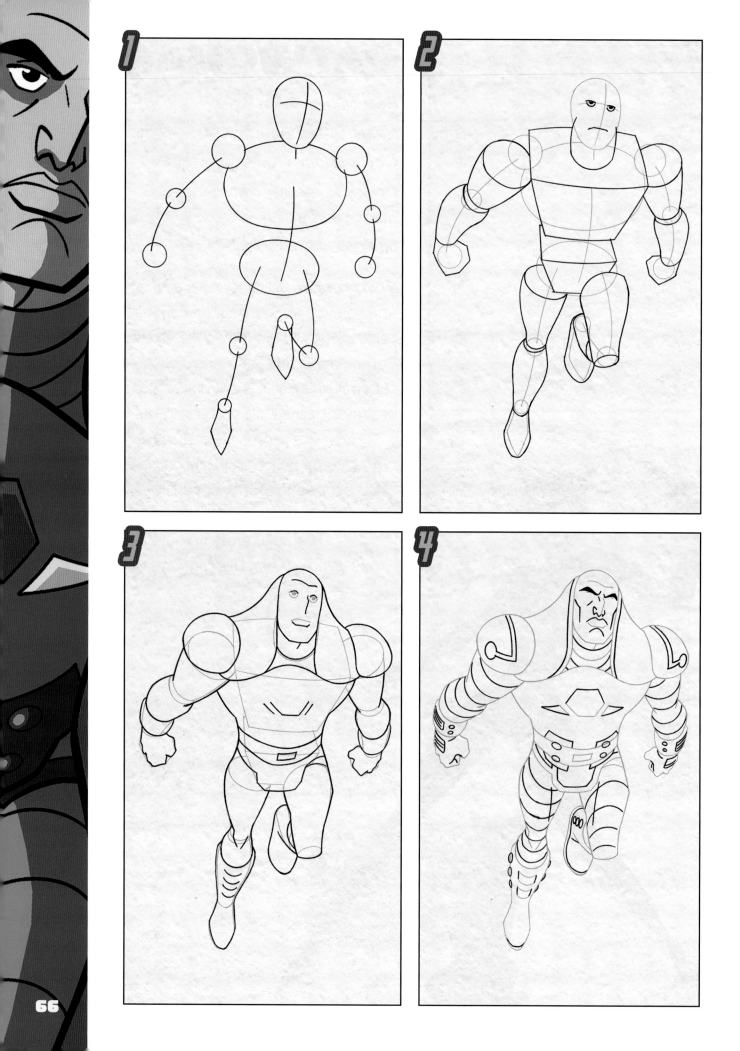

BATTLE ARMOUR LEX

Real Name: Lex Luthor

Home Base: LexCorp, Metropolis

Occupation: successful businessman, criminal mastermind

Enemy of: Superman

Abilities: scientific genius

Equipment: Kryptonite battle suit

DRAWING IDEA
Try drawing Lex battling Superman in his armour high over Metropolis!

Background: Lex Luthor is one of Metropolis' richest and most powerful people. Behind the scenes he is a criminal mastermind and a scientific genius. To deal with Superman, Lex built a Kryptonite-powered battle suit. The armoured suit gives him super-strength and allows him to fly. It's also armed with powerful Kryptonite energy weapons. While wearing his special battle suit, Lex is almost a match for Superman.

METALLO

Real Name: John Corben

Home Base: Metropolis

Occupation: criminal and super-villain

Enemy of: Superman

Abilities: enhanced strength and speed, metal transformation

Background: John Corben was a criminal who was once employed by Lex Luthor. While in prison, Luthor infected Corben with a deadly disease. To save himself, Corben agreed to an experimental medical procedure. But when he woke up, he discovered that his brain had been placed into a cyborg body powered by green Kryptonite. Now known as Metallo, he is nearly as strong and fast as Superman. The radiation from his Kryptonite heart is lethal to the Man of Steel.

DRAWING IDEA

Try drawing Metallo using his Kryptonite powers in a face-off against the Man of Steel!

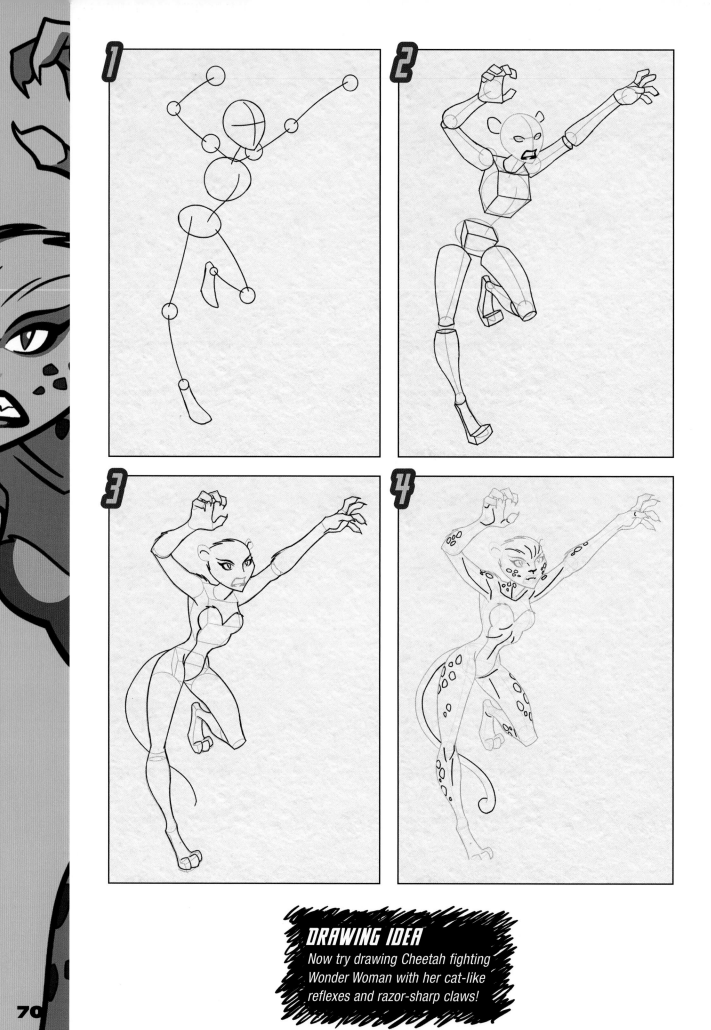

DRAWING IDEA

Now try drawing Cheetah fighting Wonder Woman with her cat-like reflexes and razor-sharp claws!

CHEETAH

Real Name: Barbara Ann Minerva

Home Base: Nottingham, UK

Occupation: biologist, professional criminal

Enemy of: Wonder Woman

Abilities: cat-like agility and reflexes, enhanced strength and speed, night vision, razor-sharp claws

Background: Dr. Barbara Ann Minerva was a biologist working on advanced genetics research. One day, she decided to test her research on herself. She was transformed into a half-human, half-cheetah hybrid. She was soon considered a freak by her fellow scientists and others. Cheetah then turned to a life of crime. She is cunning and clever, and her cat-like abilities make her a dangerous foe for Wonder Woman.

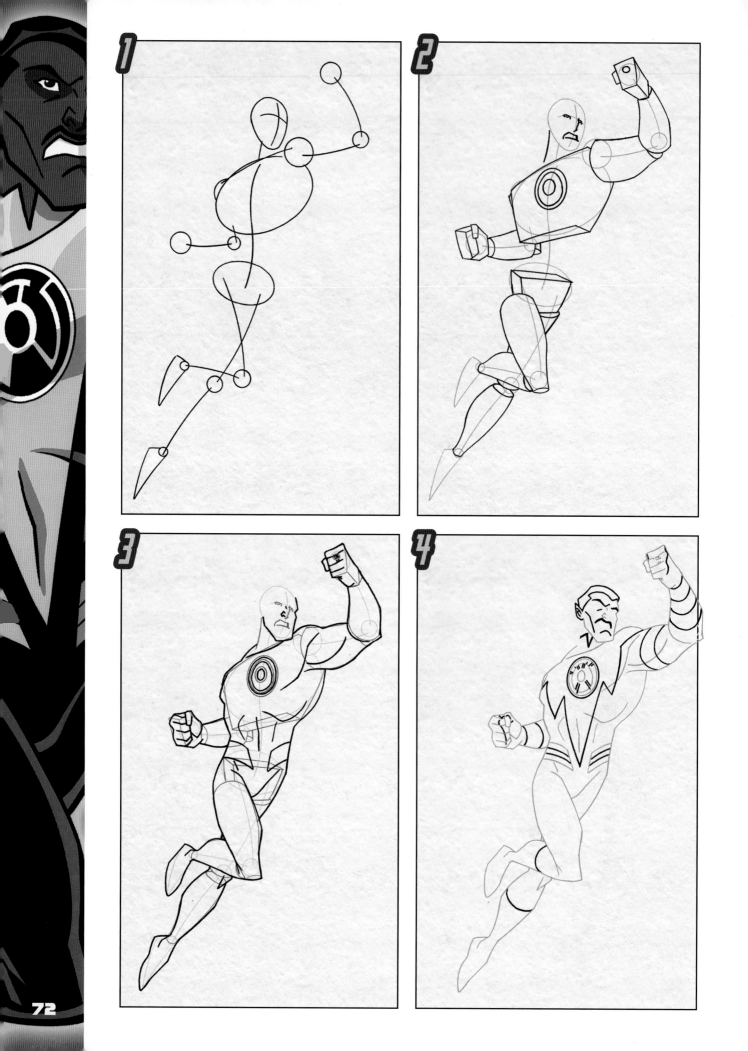

SINESTRO

Real Name: Thaal Sinestro

Home Base: Korugar, Qward

Occupation: Yellow Lantern

Enemy of: Green Lantern Corps

Abilities: military command, hand-to-hand combat skills, genius intellect

Equipment: yellow power ring

Background: Originally from the planet Korugar, Thaal Sinestro was once a famous member of the Green Lantern Corps. But he later turned to evil and became a dictator over his home planet. Sinestro was eventually captured and banished to the planet Qward. However, he later obtained a yellow power ring that was just as powerful as the Lanterns' green rings. Sinestro then formed the Sinestro Corps and swore to get his revenge against the Green Lanterns.

DRAWING IDEA
Next try drawing Sinestro creating a powerful weapon with his yellow ring to fight Green Lantern!

73

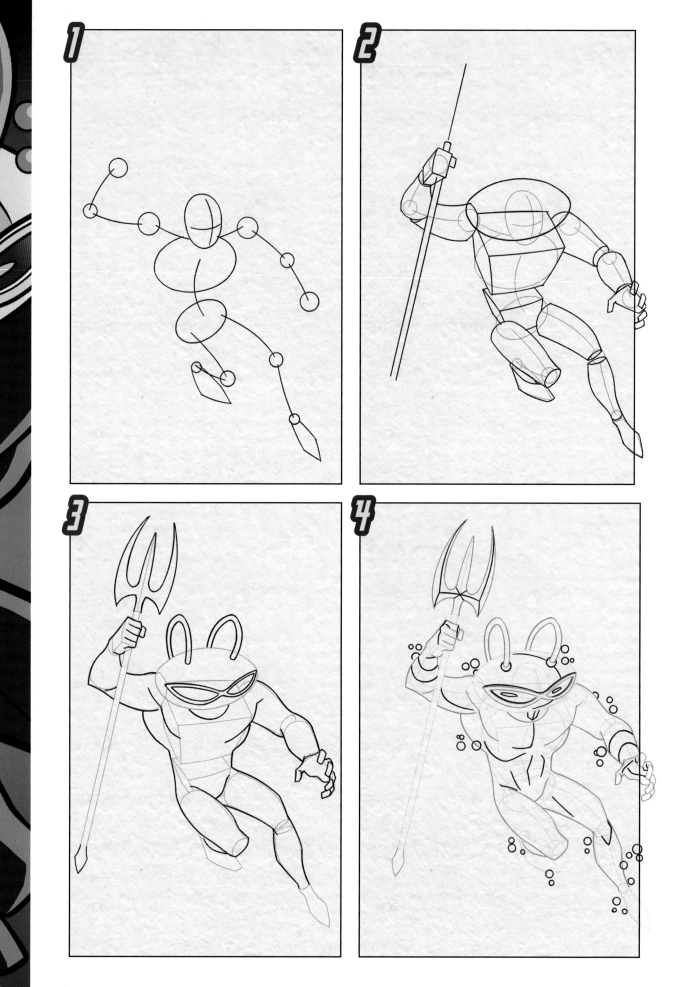

BLACK MANTA

Real Name: unknown

Home Base: the Ocean

Occupation: treasure hunter, assassin

Enemy of: Aquaman

Abilities: above-average strength and speed

Equipment: advanced diving suit, jet boots, miniature torpedoes, power helmet with infrared vision and energy beams

Background: As a young boy Black Manta was kidnapped and imprisoned on a small ship. One day, he saw Aquaman and called out for help, but the Sea King didn't hear him. At that moment the boy swore to get revenge on Aquaman. When he finally escaped, he designed a high-tech diving suit and helmet. Now Black Manta has two goals — to destroy Aquaman and to become ruler of the seas.

DRAWING IDEA
Try drawing Black Manta in an underwater fight with Aquaman and his sea creature friends!

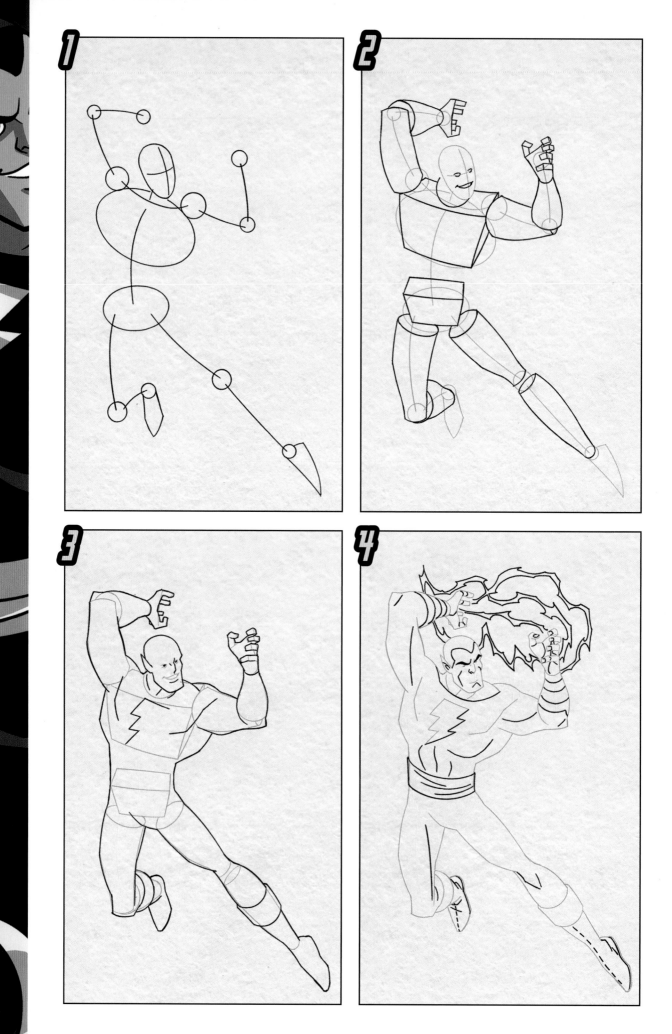

BLACK ADAM

Real Name: Teth-Adam

Home Base: Kahndaq

Occupation: dictator

Enemy of: SHAZAM!

Abilities: superhuman strength, speed and stamina; enhanced intelligence; accelerated healing; flight; invulnerability

DRAWING IDEA
Try drawing Black Adam using his magical powers to battle his arch-enemy SHAZAM!

Background: Teth-Adam was once a fair and honest prince. The wizard Shazam gave him the powers of the gods Shu, Heru, Amon, Zehuti, Aton and Mehen. But Adam later became a cruel dictator. Eventually, the wizard trapped Adam's soul and powers inside a magic necklace. However, the necklace was later discovered by Adam's descendant, Theo Adam. Now Black Adam's powers and memories live on through Theo. Only SHAZAM! can stop the super-villain's goal of ruling the world.

SUPER-VILLAINS UNITED

Super-villains usually like to work alone. However, being a successful criminal can be difficult with super heroes around. To gain an advantage, villains sometimes form secret groups to fight their enemies together. These groups have had several names including the Secret Society of Super-Villains, the Injustice League and the Legion of Doom. Villains can be powerful and dangerous when they team up. But luckily, villains have a fatal flaw — they usually don't work well together. They often end up fighting with each other instead of the heroes they hate!

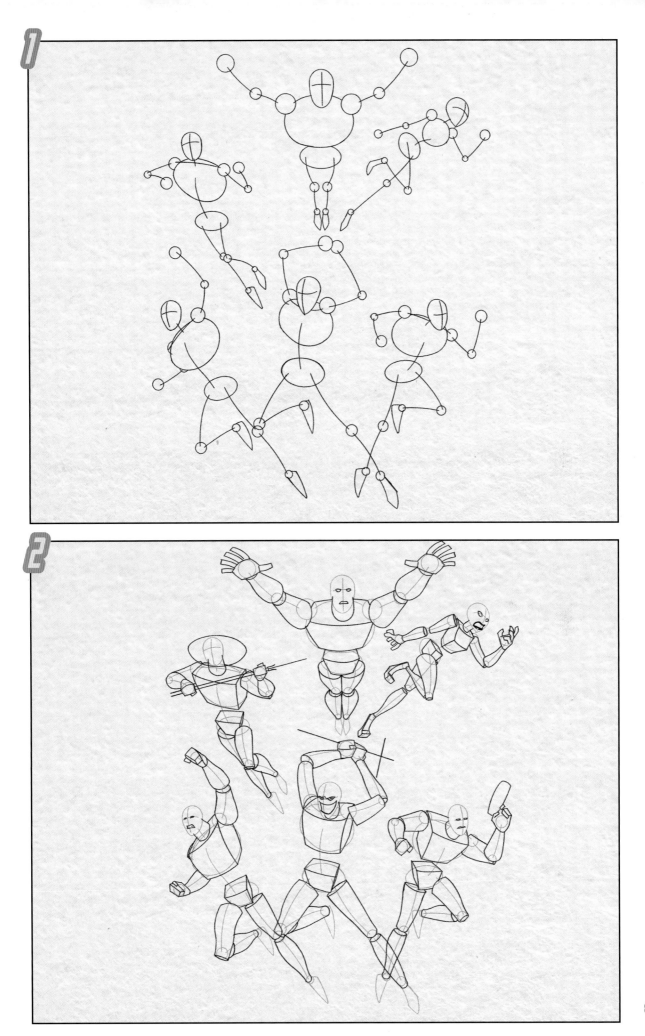

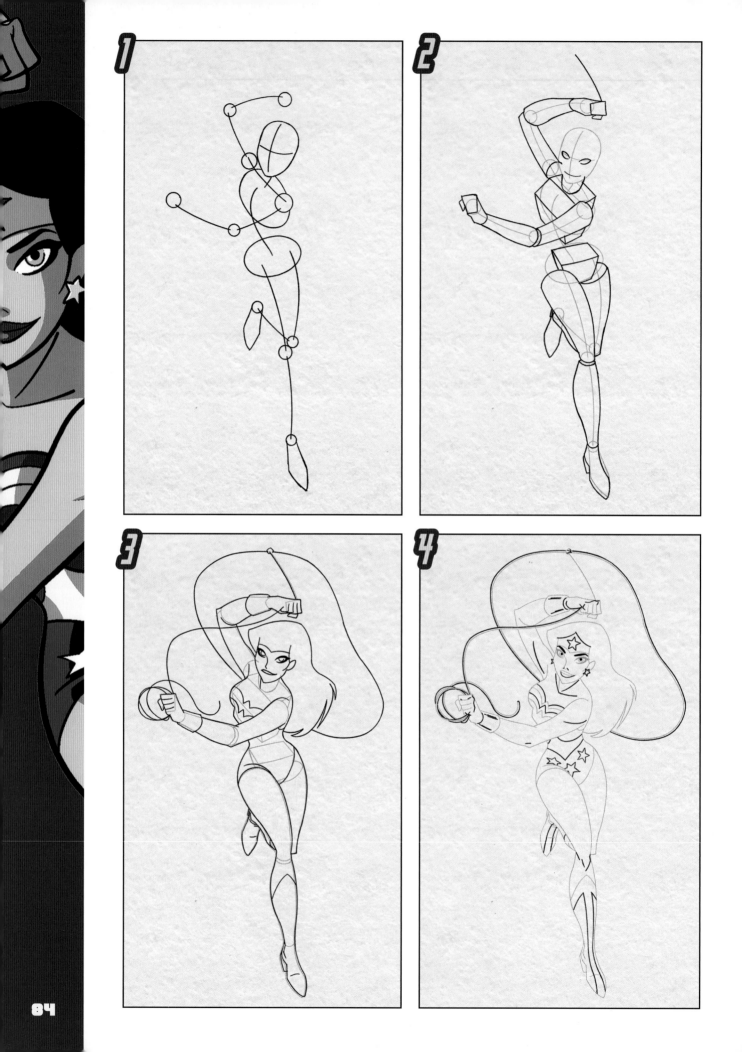

DRAWING IDEA
Try drawing Wonder Woman battling her arch-enemy Cheetah!

WONDER WOMAN

Real Name: Princess Diana

Home Base: Island of Themyscira

Occupation: Amazonian princess, crime fighter

Abilities: super-strength and speed, flight

Equipment: indestructible bracelets, magical tiara, Lasso of Truth

Background: Diana is the Princess of Themyscira, the hidden home of the Amazons. As she grew up, Diana knew she could be more than just an Amazonian princess. She trained hard and became highly skilled in hand-to-hand combat. Now, with her magical tiara, indestructible bracelets and Lasso of Truth, Diana fights the forces of evil as Wonder Woman.

GREEN LANTERN

Real Name: Hal Jordan

Home Base: Coast City

Occupation: test pilot, intergalactic police officer

Abilities: green energy weapons and force fields, flight

Equipment: green power ring

Background: Hal Jordan was a brash and reckless test pilot for Ferris Aircraft. One day he discovered the severely injured alien Abin Sur in his crashed spaceship. Before he died, Abin Sur gave Hal his Green Lantern power ring. He believed that Hal had the strength of will needed to be part of the Green Lantern Corps. Using the ring's powerful green energy, Hal can create any type of weapon or force field that he can imagine to protect Earth from the forces of evil.

DRAWING IDEA
Next try drawing Green Lantern creating a giant green boxing glove with his ring to knock out some villains!

1

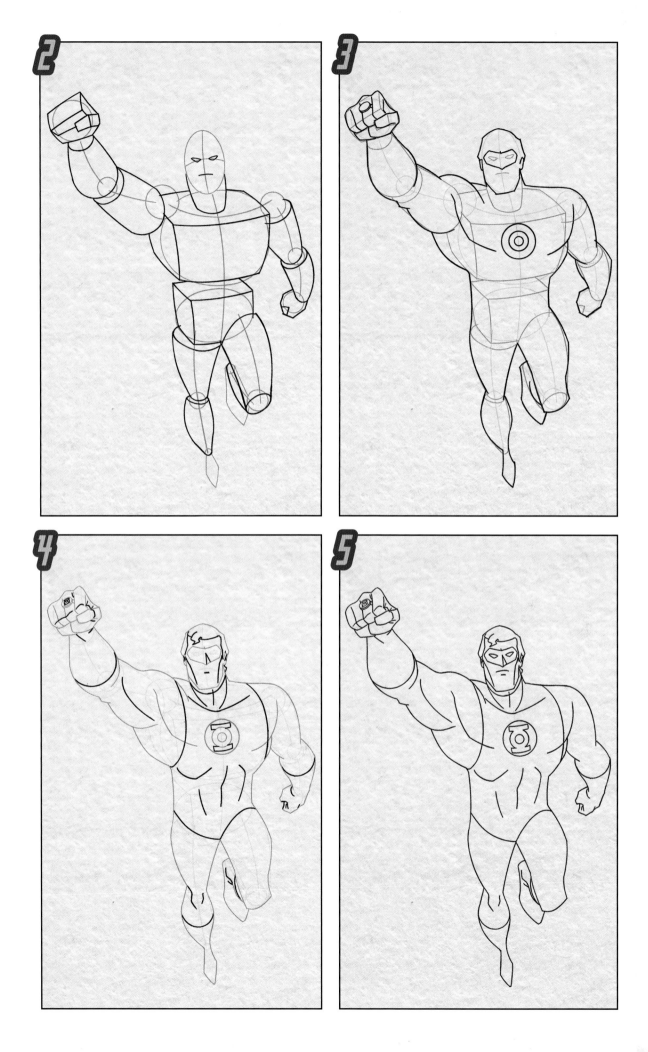

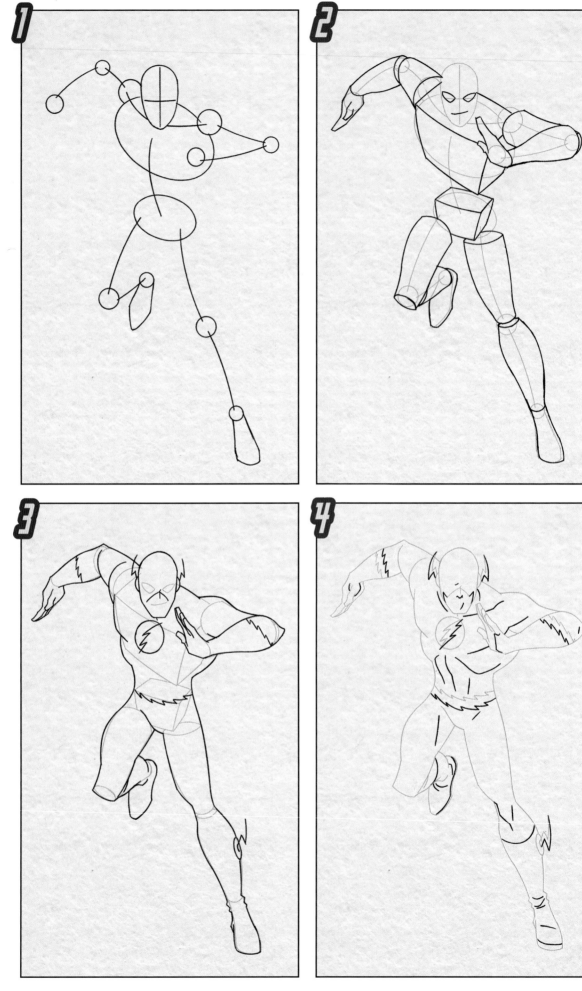

5

DRAWING IDEA

Try drawing The Flash outrunning the icy rays from Captain Cold's gun!

THE FLASH

Real Name: Barry Allen

Home Base: Central City

Occupation: forensic scientist, crime fighter

Abilities: super-speed, accelerated healing, phasing

Background: Forensic scientist Barry Allen was working in his lab one stormy night when a powerful bolt of lightning shot through a window. The lightning destroyed a chemical cabinet, soaking Barry in electrified chemicals. Shortly after the accident Barry discovered he could move at supersonic speeds. He can even vibrate his body so fast that he can phase right through solid walls! As The Flash, Barry uses his super-speed to save people from danger and to stop criminals in their tracks.

5

DRAWING IDEA
Next try drawing Green Arrow using his trick arrows to stop a criminal's getaway car!

GREEN ARROW

Real Name: Oliver "Ollie" Queen

Home Base: Star City

Occupation: billionaire businessman and politician, crime fighter

Abilities: expert marksmanship, hand-to-hand combat skills

Equipment: trick arrows

Background: As a boy, Oliver Queen was skilled with a bow, and his hero was Robin Hood. When Ollie's parents were killed, he grew into a rich and spoiled thrill-seeker who cared only for himself. But that all changed one day when he was stranded on a small island. There, he learned to survive by honing his fighting skills and becoming a master archer. After being rescued, Oliver decided to change his ways. He now models himself on his childhood hero. He dresses in green and uses his amazing archery skills to keep crime off the streets of Star City.

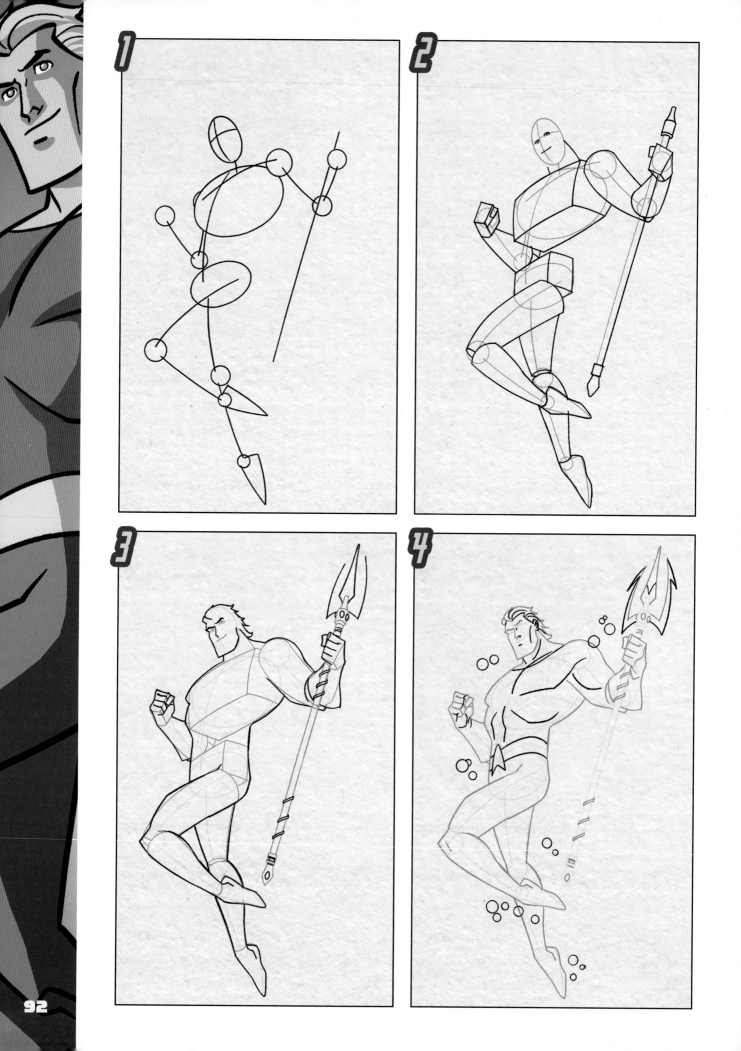

DRAWING IDEA
Try drawing Aquaman communicating with some sea creatures to stop Black Manta's evil plans!

5

AQUAMAN

Real Name: Arthur Curry

Home Base: Atlantis

Occupation: King of Atlantis, protector of the oceans

Abilities: super-strength and speed, underwater breathing, telepathic communication

Background: Arthur Curry grew up as the son of a lighthouse keeper. At a young age, Arthur learned he could breathe under water and talk to fish and other sea creatures. Eventually Arthur learned that his mother was the Queen of Atlantis and that he would one day be a king. When he grew up, Arthur decided to use his powers to defend Earth's oceans and wildlife and help to stop the world's worst villains.

DRAWING IDEA
Next try drawing J'onn J'onzz taking the shape of a powerful animal to help Green Lantern defeat Sinestro!

MARTIAN MANHUNTER

Real Name: J'onn J'onzz

Home Base: Mars, Justice League Watchtower

Occupation: detective, Martian police officer

Abilities: super-strength and speed; flight; telepathy; shape-shifting; investigation skills

Background: When powerful aliens invaded Mars, the Martian race was nearly wiped out. As the last survivor, J'onn J'onzz managed to escape and fled to Earth. There he joined Earth's mightiest heroes to defeat the alien threat. Afterwards, J'onn decided to make Earth his new home. Using his shape-shifting ability, J'onn blends in with Earth's people. He uses his telepathic powers and detective skills to solve crimes and stop villains' wicked plans.

CYBORG

Real Name: Victor "Vic" Stone

Home Base: Justice League Watchtower, Science and Technology Advanced Research (S.T.A.R.) Labs

Occupation: student athlete, crime fighter

Abilities: super-strength and speed, able to link with computers

Equipment: enhanced cybernetic systems

Background: Victor "Vic" Stone was visiting his father at the local S.T.A.R. Lab when he was horribly injured in an accident. Vic's father saved his life by replacing much of his body with cybernetic parts. Vic's new body gives him superhuman abilities, and he can link with almost any computer in the world. Vic once dreamed of becoming a star athlete. But now he has a new purpose — to fight crime as one of the world's greatest heroes.

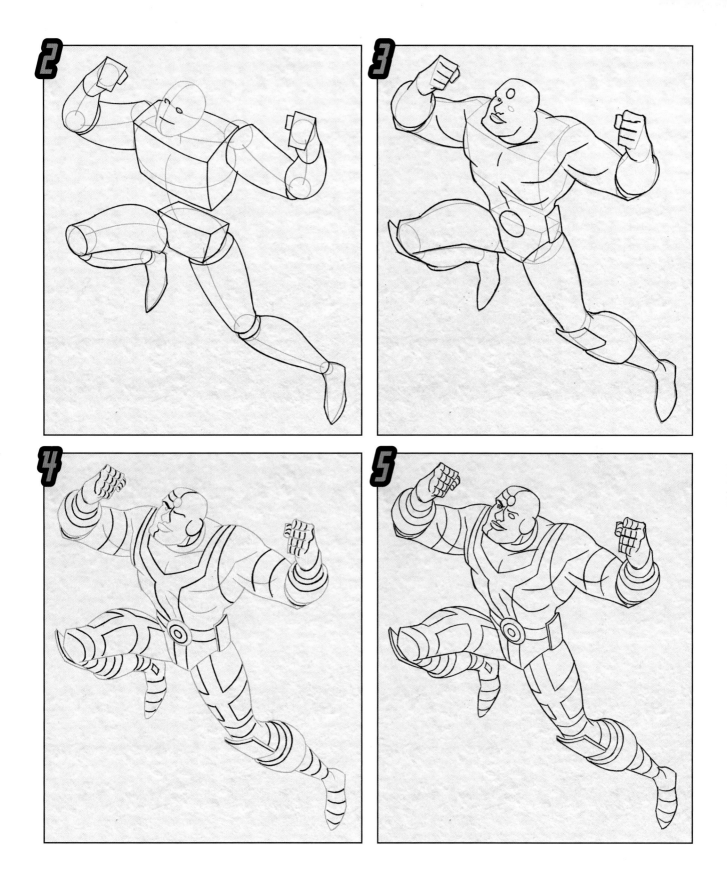

DRAWING IDEA

Try drawing Cyborg lifting a smashed car to save someone trapped underneath it.

1

DRAWING IDEA
Next draw Black Canary using her special ability to help Green Arrow stop a bank robbery!

BLACK CANARY

Real Name: Dinah Lance

Home Base: Gotham City

Occupation: adventurer, crime fighter

Abilities: martial arts expert, ultrasonic "Canary Cry" scream

Background: Dinah Lance comes from a family of crime fighters. Her father is a police officer, and her mother fought crime as the original Black Canary. Her mother didn't want her to become a crime fighter, but Dinah followed in her mother's footsteps anyway. However, Dinah has a special ability of her own. Her ultrasonic "Canary Cry" scream can stun foes, damage objects and even shatter metal!

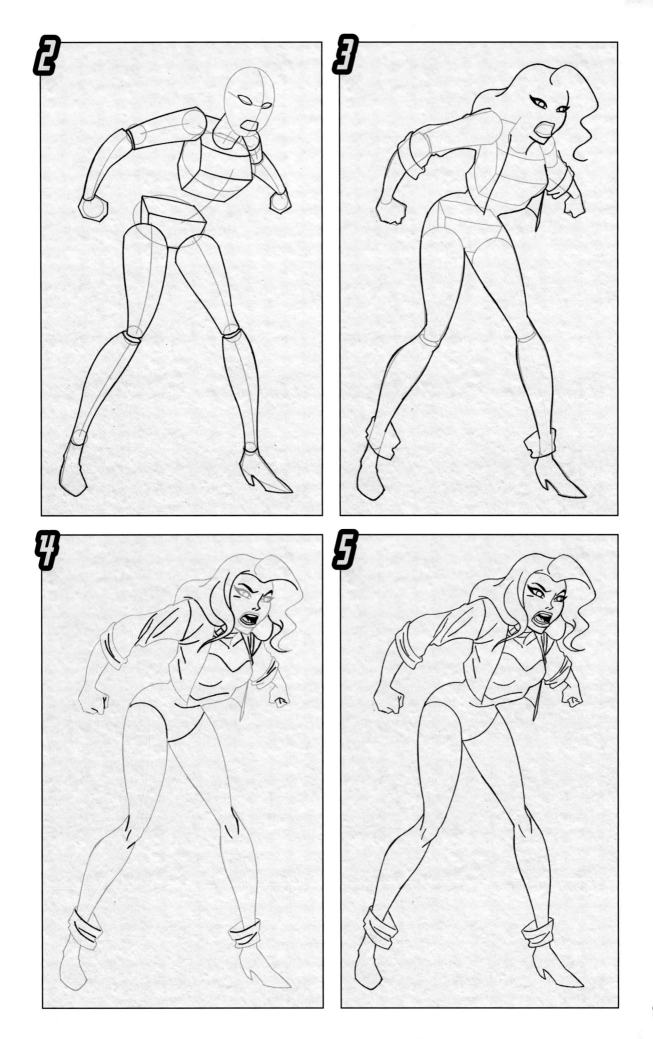

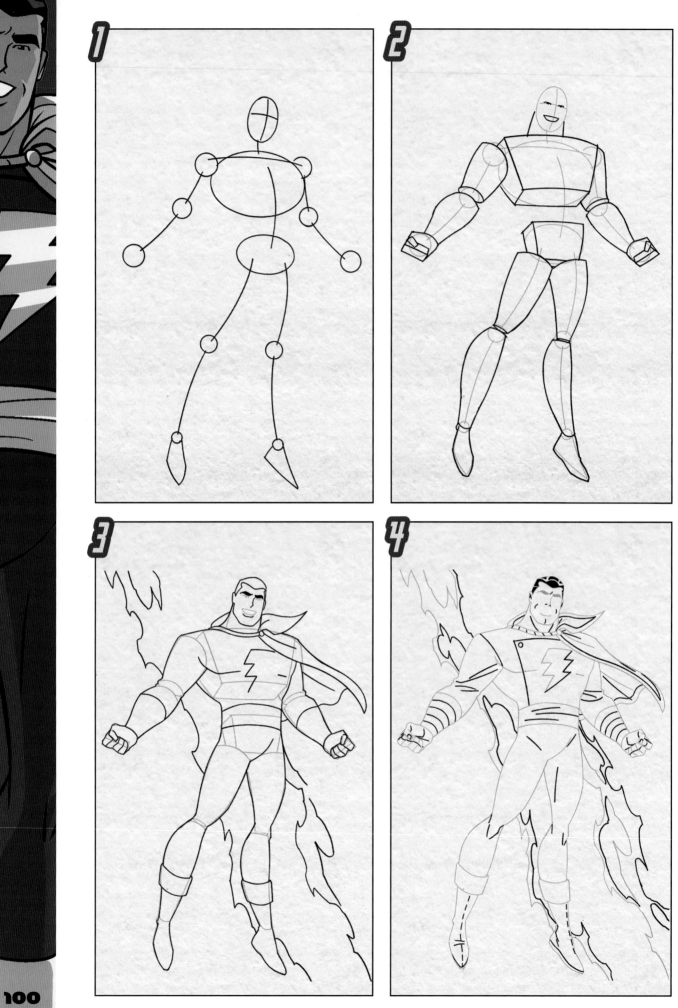

SHAZAM!

Real Name: William "Billy" Batson

Home Base: Fawcett City

Occupation: student, reporter, super hero

Abilities: super-strength, speed and stamina; flight; invulnerability

Background: Young Billy Batson's parents were killed during an archaeological expedition to Egypt. The powerful wizard Shazam soon learned about Billy and his strong sense of justice. The wizard gave Billy the powers of several historical figures. These included: the wisdom of Solomon, the strength of Hercules, the stamina of Atlas, the power of Zeus, the courage of Achilles and the speed of Mercury. Now, when Billy calls out the magic word "SHAZAM!," he is transformed into a mighty hero who is almost as powerful as Superman!

DRAWING IDEA
Try drawing SHAZAM! fighting his arch-enemy Black Adam to stop him from taking over the world!

DRAWING IDEA
Try drawing Supergirl fighting alongside Superman to stop Brainiac from destroying Earth!

SUPERGIRL

Real Name: Kara Zor-El

Home Base: Metropolis

Occupation: student, super hero

Abilities: super-strength, speed and hearing; X-ray vision; heat vision; flight; invulnerability

Background: Kara Zor-El is Superman's cousin and the last survivor of Krypton's Argo City. Like Kal-El, Kara was sent to Earth in a spacecraft. Superman took Kara to live with the Kents as their teenage niece. The Kents taught her the same values they had taught Clark. Meanwhile, Superman taught her how to control her new-found abilities. Eventually Kara moved to Metropolis to fight crime as Supergirl.

5

DRAWING IDEA
Now try drawing Nightwing using his acrobatic skills to take on a group of thugs on the street!

NIGHTWING

Real Name: Dick Grayson

Home Base: Blüdhaven

Occupation: adventurer, crime fighter

Abilities: master of martial arts and acrobatics, master detective

Equipment: pair of fighting sticks

Background: As a boy, Dick Grayson was a member of the Flying Graysons: a family of circus acrobats. When Dick's parents were killed in a tragic accident, Bruce Wayne took in the heartbroken boy. When Dick learned that Bruce was secretly also Batman, he began training to become the first Robin. Batman and Robin spent several years fighting crime together as the Dynamic Duo. But when Dick grew up, he struck out on his own. He created a new suit for himself and moved to a new city. Now he protects the streets of Blüdhaven as the acrobatic crime fighter, Nightwing.

THE JUSTICE LEAGUE

When Earth was invaded by powerful aliens, even the world's mightiest heroes were unable to defeat them on their own. Only by joining together did they have the strength to overcome the alien threat. After stopping the invasion, Superman, Batman, Wonder Woman, Green Lantern, The Flash and Martian Manhunter formed the Justice League. The heroes then built the Watchtower, a space station that orbits Earth. From here, the Justice League can watch over Earth and launch powerful defences to protect its people.

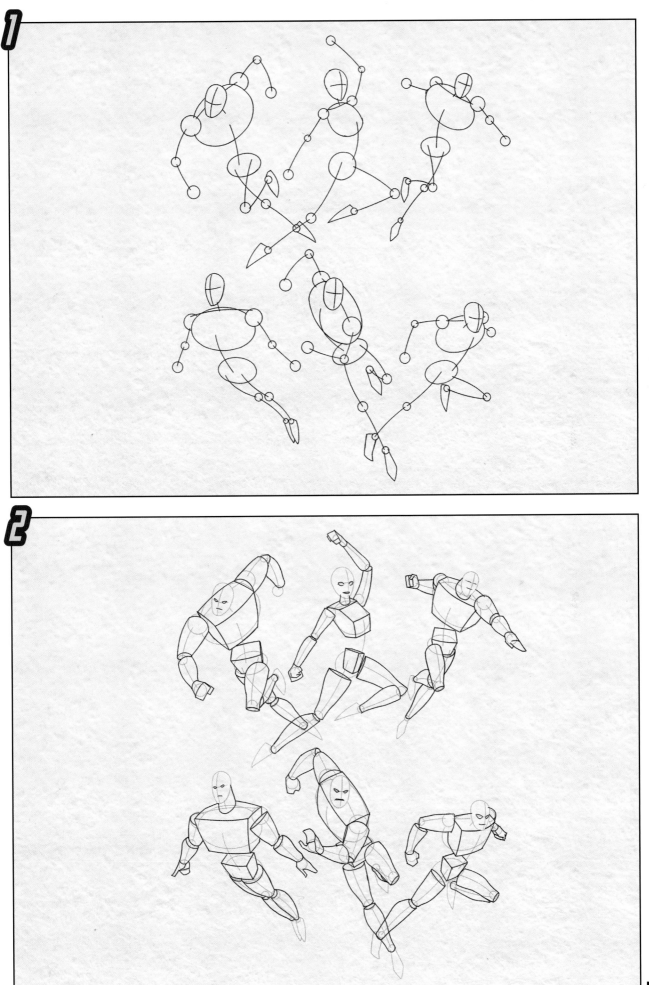

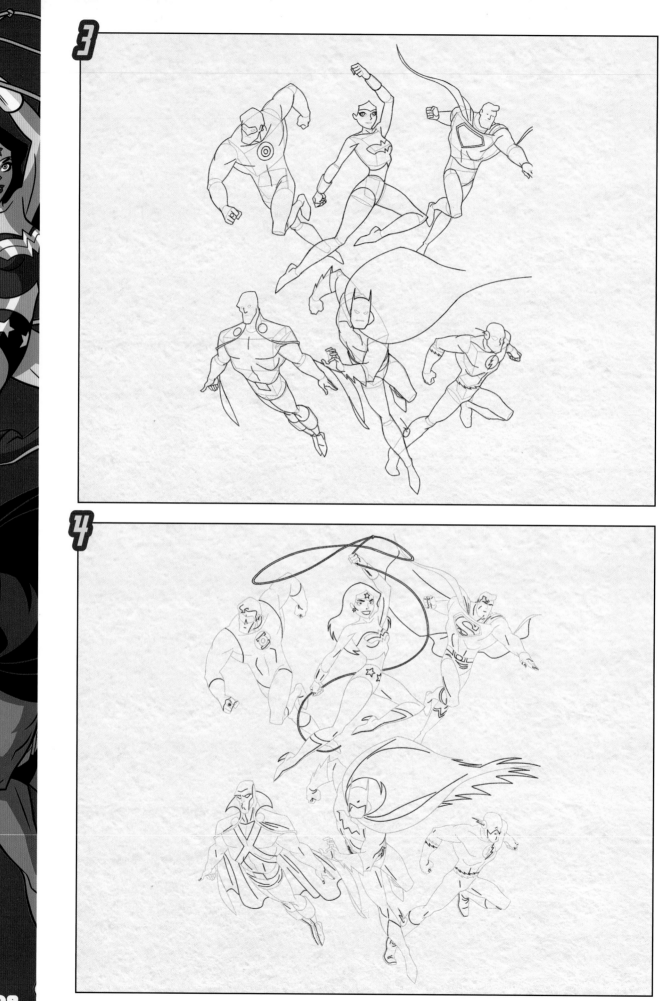

5

5

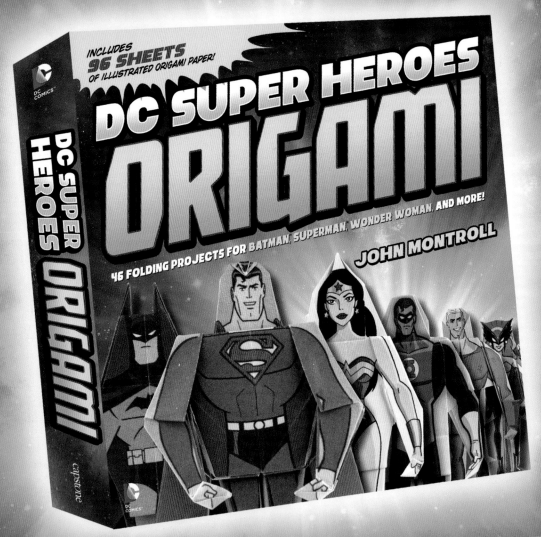

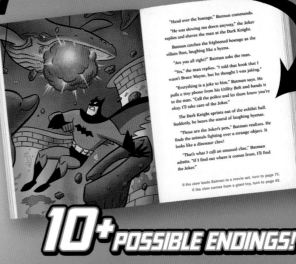
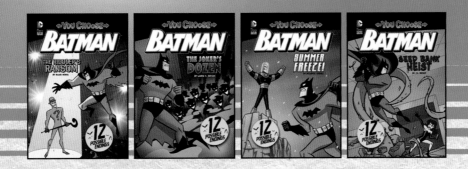

Published in 2015 by Curious Fox, an imprint of Capstone Global Library Limited,
7 Pilgrim Street, London, EC4V 6LB – Registered company number: 6695582

www.curious-fox.com

Design Elements:
Capstone Studio: Karon Dubke; Shutterstock: Artishok, Bennyartist, Eliks, gst,
Mazzzur, Roobcio

ISBN 978 1 782 02452 1
19 18 17 16 15
10 9 8 7 6 5 4 3 2 1

A CIP catalogue for this book is available from the British Library.

Printed and bound in China

For Daniel and Isabelle – the coolest super heroes I'll ever know!
– A. Sautter